Solutions for Impact Investors:

From Strategy to Implementation

Steven Godeke
Raúl Pomares

with

Albert V. Bruno
Pat Guerra
Charly Kleissner
Hersh Shefrin

Original © November 2009, Rockefeller Philanthropy Advisors
Reprinted with minor updates August 2010

ISBN 978-1-61658-210-4

table of contents

foreword

Since we published *Philanthropy's New Passing Gear: Mission-Related Investing* in early 2008, the investment and philanthropic landscape has changed dramatically. Despite the global economic volatility we have seen in the past year, and perhaps in part a result of it, interest in impact investing — creating social and environmental impacts in addition to investment returns — has grown significantly. Investors are creatively challenging the status quo in order to address major problems such as poverty, climate change and the inequality between rich and poor.

While organizations serving the needs of investors and philanthropists interested in this approach have begun to multiply, and new tools are being developed to provide insights into how people and markets interact, barriers still exist. There is a clear need for established best practices and for practical guidance in developing an asset allocation framework; sourcing investment opportunities; performing due diligence on managers and opportunities; understanding the behavioral and external factors that motivate investment decisions; analyzing risk and return from a financial, social and environmental perspective; as well as measuring and benchmarking the performance and impact of these types of investments.

The pathways to scaling social and environmental innovation are also changing. Collaborations among the public, private and social sectors have proliferated as governments have responded to the current financial crisis and sought to find innovative means to address these challenges. While philanthropy has always relied on other sectors to co-create and sustain social change, the fact remains that governments and traditional philanthropy do not have sufficient funds to address the world's most serious problems. Commercial capital and the tremendous power of market forces will have to be part of the solution.

Solutions for Impact Investors: From Strategy to Implementation aims to increase the rigor with which impact investors frame their investment decisions and demonstrate the integration of impact investing across asset classes. In conjunction with the team of academics and practitioners who have produced this monograph, Rockefeller Philanthropy Advisors highlights some of the areas in which behavioral economics and innovative organizational and legal structures can be applied to the discipline of impact investing. By describing best practices in transparency, disclosure and rigorous decision-making, we also hope to bridge the divide between traditional and social purpose investing.

We believe impact investing will continue to play a central role in creating positive social change. The need for impact and rigor will become more, rather than less important. Underlying factors such as wealth creation, vast generational transfers of wealth, efficiency and leverage will remain. Impact investors are continuing to build the field by doing a better and innovative job of generating positive social change as well as devising ways to leverage more of their assets toward these efforts. We hope you will be inspired by these tools and stories to seek out opportunities to apply impact investing to bring more capital to bear on addressing the pressing social and environmental challenges of our time.

Kevin P.A. Broderick
Chair, Board of Directors

Melissa A. Berman
President & CEO
Rockefeller Philanthropy Advisors, October 2009

acknowledgements

The authors wish to thank everyone who helped inform and inspire this publication. We especially extend our gratitude to our advisory council — a passionate group of impact investors, academics and practitioners. This guide would not have been possible without their invaluable input and support.

- Doug Bauer, Executive Director, The Clark Foundation;
- Antony Bugg-Levine, Managing Director, the Rockefeller Foundation;
- Mark Campanale, Director, Halloran Philanthropies;
- Sam Collin, Charity Adviser, EIRIS Foundation;
- Lisa Hagerman, Director, More for Mission Campaign Resource Center;
- Al Hammond, Senior Entrepreneur, Ashoka;
- Pamela Hartigan, Director, Skoll Centre for Social Entrepreneurship at Oxford Said Business School;
- Harry Hummels, Professor of Economics and Business Administration at Universiteit Maastricht;
- Steven Lydenberg, Chief Investment Officer, Domini Social Investments and Vice President of the Domini Funds;
- Preston D. Pinkett III, Vice President, Social Investment Program, Prudential Financial;
- Meir Statman, Glenn Klimek Professor of Finance at Santa Clara University;
- Georgette Wong, Principal, Correlation Consulting; and
- David Wood, Director, The Institute for Responsible Investment.

We also wish to thank the following colleagues who helped develop case studies and review the text: Shari Berenbach, Melissa Berman, Candi Deschamps, Julian Himes, Koert Jansen, Robert Katz, Tracy Palandjian, Carl Palmer, Luther Ragin, Jr., Ravi Shankar, Gary Schick, Don Shaffer, Gary Sprague, Doug Stamm, Bill Tarr, Joan Trant, Brian Trelstad and Rosa Wang.

Hasani Sinclair served as lead researcher for the impact investment profiles featured in this guide and on RPA's Web site; and Rob Steiner contributed to the final format and content of these profiles.

The authors received strong editorial support from Lisa Kleissner and Lauren Russell Geskos. The book was beautifully designed and produced by Art270. Patricia Holland Design contributed to the design of many of the graphics.

We would like to extend special thanks to Charly and Lisa Kleissner from the KL Felicitas Foundation; Antony Bugg-Levine and Brinda Ganguly from the Rockefeller Foundation; Russ Hall and Alan Marty from Legacy Works; Jesse Fink from the Betsy and Jesse Fink Foundation; Stuart Davidson from the Woodcock Foundation; and Steve Toben from the Flora Family Foundation. Without their enthusiasm and support, this publication would not have been possible. We are grateful for their commitment to impact investing and to broadly disseminating its potential to as wide an audience as possible. This work also builds on the pioneering work of the F.B. Heron Foundation.

Finally, please let us know what you think. Please send any comments or feedback to info@rockpa.org. We hope you find the guide useful and meaningful to the important work of moving more capital into impact investments.

— *The Authors*

Chapter 1:
Introduction

From Strategy to Implementation: How can our investments make a difference? How can we maximize our impact?

"Impact Investing seeks to generate social and environmental impacts in addition to financial returns."

As we look out at the challenges facing the world and the limits of the current resources addressing them, we see impact investing playing a central role in bringing forward real solutions. We believe impact investing can create social good at scale and begin to address some of the world's most pressing problems where commercial markets and donor-based programs have not. The sharp dichotomy between profit-maximizing financial investment and "give-it-away" charity is gradually losing its edge. Jed Emerson has used the term "Blended Value Investing" to describe this combination of investment and philanthropy. He concisely framed the concept in the following:

"There is an idea that values are divided between the financial and the societal, but this is a fundamentally wrong way to view how we create value. Value is whole. The world is not divided into corporate bad guys and social heroes."[1]

However, if we want to ensure that our good intentions create real impact, these aspirations must be supported by a well-considered investment strategy and a rigorous execution process. Impact investors are now able to execute strategies across a range of asset classes, risk-adjusted financial returns and impact themes — these investors face the challenge of selecting outstanding impact investments directly or indirectly through the appropriate funds which, in turn, evaluate and select the impact investments. Given the growing opportunities in today's marketplace, these strategies can and should be driven by an impact investor's dual goals of addressing specific social and/or environmental impacts while seeking an appropriate level of investment return. Our team of academics and impact investment practitioners set out to explore the structures and processes impact investors can use to tighten the link between investment decision-making and generation of impact. We have chosen the broader term "impact investing" in this monograph since its relevance extends to individual and institutional investors in addition to philanthropic investors such as foundations where mission-related investment would describe this activity.

As we seek to create impact and investment return simultaneously, the framing is critical. By clarifying our definitions of investment and impact, we can better understand some of the assumptions and views people bring to this field.

Impact: a meaningful change in economic, social, cultural, environmental and/or political conditions due to specific actions and behavioral changes by individuals, communities and/or society as a whole.[2]

Chapter 1: Introduction

Investment: the choice by an investor to risk his or her assets with the goal of a financial gain in the future.

Are these two objectives at cross-purposes? Must we sacrifice return in order to generate impact, or conversely, must we dilute impact to gain additional financial return? Is there a middle ground between creating dependencies through grantmaking and sacrificing long-term sustainability to achieve short-term financial returns? Or can pursuing both objectives result in enhanced financial returns with a meaningful impact?

Impact Investor Categories: Commercial and Philanthropic

Impact investors can approach the question of financial return and impact very differently. Traditionally, impact investors such as US-based public pension funds have been restricted to making only market-rate investments due to their understanding of their fiduciary responsibilities. Similarly, a foundation's charitable status may drive it to make below-market impact investments. High net-worth individuals and families may use multiple avenues to pursue their impact investment objectives. In the recent impact investing report by the Monitor Institute,[3] the authors coined the terms "Financial First" and "Impact First" to describe this distinction:

1. *Financial First Investors seek to optimize financial returns with a floor for social/environmental impact. This group tends to consist of commercial investors who search for sub-sectors that offer market-rate returns while yielding some social/environmental good.*

These investors may be driven by fiduciary requirements as in the case of pension plans.

2. ***Impact First Investors*** *seek to optimize social or environmental returns with a financial floor. This group uses social/environmental good as a primary objective and may accept a range of returns, from principal to market-rate. This group is able to take a lower than market-rate of return in order to seed new investment funds that may be perceived as higher risk, or to reach tougher social/ environmental goals that cannot be achieved in combination with market-rates of return.*

Looking across the universe of impact investors, it is important to keep this distinction in mind in order to understand the investment opportunities specific impact investors will pursue. However, investors may also make both financial first and impact first investments. This clear separation between financial returns and impact may be less appropriate for investors who use a broader, more integrated approach — including both financial and non-financial factors — when evaluating their investment opportunities.

The Target Audiences

Solutions for Impact Investors: From Strategy to Implementation is written from the perspective of the impact investor supplying the capital rather than the enterprises using the capital. Our expected audience includes investors who may have already made impact investments, but have not yet connected these investments to their overall investment strategy, and traditional investors who have not made impact investments and struggle with how impact investing can be integrated into pre-existing asset allocation and portfolio management models. While we acknowledge the important role which grant-based philanthropy can play in furthering social and environmental goals, it is not the focus of this monograph. Interested readers include:

- Philanthropic investors seeking to enhance their knowledge of social, mission-related and program-related investments;
- Individual investors (e.g., high net-worth individuals);
- Institutional investors (e.g., pension fund managers); and
- Advisors (wealth management advisors, investment advisors and family trust advisors) seeking to provide their clients with impact investment opportunities.

Publication Goals

In writing this monograph, our main goal is to provide impact investors with tools to tighten the link between their investment decisions and impact creation. Our intent is threefold: to attract more capital to impact investing; to assist impact investors as they move from organizational change to executing and refining their impact investment decision-making process; and to narrow the gap within foundations between program professionals and investment professionals thereby contributing to a mutual understanding and implementation of a portfolio approach to impact investing.

Additionally, we intend to help break down the barriers making it difficult to identify opportunities in impact investing. To this end, we provide examples throughout the monograph and at www.rockpa.org/impactinvesting of impact investment opportunities in most major asset classes.

While we understand the important role that impact investors can play in providing financial capital, we also want to acknowledge the wide range of non-financial resources needed to address the world's problems. Our intent with this monograph is not to provide a comprehensive list of investments across asset classes nor any type of investment advice with regard to the selected profiles. We strongly encourage the reader to conduct their own assessment and evaluation for risk and suitability before considering any investment.

Beyond the Tyranny of OR

In the business bestseller, *Built to Last*,[4] author Jim Collins emphasizes the importance of companies avoiding what he called the "Tyranny of OR" and encouraged them to harness the "Genius of AND" when making business decisions. He cites some of the characteristics of *Built To Last* companies:

- Purpose beyond profit AND pragmatic pursuit of profit;
- Clear vision & sense of direction AND opportunistic experimentation;
- Audacious goals AND incremental evolutionary progress;
- Selection of managers steeped in the core activities of the firm AND selection of managers that induce change; and
- Investments for the long-term AND demands for short-term performance.

We believe successful impact investing is based on moving beyond a similar false assumption that investors must choose between social and environmental impact OR financial return. Specifically, we believe that an impact investor can benefit from:

Chapter 1: Introduction

- Creating new impact-related processes AND operating within strict investment policy discipline;
- Optimizing for environmental & social impact AND applying the rigor of investment management tools;
- Investing in new markets & asset classes AND maintaining exposure to traditional investment strategies;
- Embracing new business models AND adhering to recognized financial theory;
- Evaluating impact performance AND subjecting investments to recognized financial benchmarks; and
- Expanding the scope and scale of philanthropic capital AND maintaining adherence to fiduciary responsibilities.

Throughout this monograph, we illustrate how the impact investor can embrace the Genius of AND to successfully develop and execute a rigorous approach, utilizing existing portfolio theory and investment discipline.

Uncertainty and Risk

The generation of investment returns and impact requires us to take actions we hope will deliver positive social and financial returns in the future. Whether making a loan or funding a program, this desired future outcome is subject to risk. We must understand that both investing and generating impact operates under uncertainty. Given this uncertainty, we need to stay alert to both the societal changes we seek and the changing investment environment and formulate clear investment policies to express our risk preferences and ensure well-informed and focused investment decisions.

Behavioral Finance and Impact Investing

In addition to embedding impact investing within the traditional investment framework of risk and return, we would like to explore how elements of behavioral finance can be applied to the discipline of impact investing. Traditional finance uses models in which people are self-interested and rational. While this framework is appealingly simple, evidence from psychology, economics and finance indicates that both assumptions are unrealistic. People can be altruistic and less than fully rational. With the study of rationality, the behavioral finance literature emphasizes that both investors and managers of firms deal with the real world complexity of financial markets by relying on rules of thumb known as heuristics. These influences typically cause investors and managers to be subject to specific biases. These biases seem to contradict Adam Smith's concept that an "invisible hand" efficiently allocates resources in competitive markets. This invisible hand conclusion is derived under special conditions in which externalities and public goods are absent and information is freely available to all. We now understand that these are unrealistic conditions and that the presence of externalities, public goods and imperfect information can lead to inefficiencies known as market failures.

Impact investors can also make mistakes, accepting tradeoffs whereby they misjudge either the social benefits generated by the investment or its full costs. In this regard, the lessons of behavioral finance apply as much to impact investors as to others. Here are a few lessons from behavioral finance that impact investors might keep in mind:

• Recognize your cognitive limitations;
• Making the absolute best decision is an unrealistic goal.

Economics Nobel laureate Herbert Simon pointed out that

most of us 'satisfice' rather than optimize, meaning that we are content with decisions that achieve some goal with which we shall be satisfied, rather than delaying a decision until we find the absolute best alternative;

- Recognize that you, and others, will be relying on rules of thumb to make your decisions; and
- Recognize that the challenge is to find sensible rules of thumb. Indeed, one goal of this monograph is to provide sensible heuristics for impact investing.

Throughout the monograph we highlight behavioral finance issues, how they affect investment decisions, and how these issues can be addressed in the context of impact investing. Along with specific guidelines, we also provide general suggestions for mitigating bias. Finally, we help investors develop a menu of sensible behavioral finance questions to assist in the investment evaluation process.

Challenges Ahead

Translating impact investing from a concept into action raises several challenges we wish to address:

- How do impact investors formulate a strategy to support their mission and values and then find the appropriate investment opportunities to realize that strategy?
- How are impact investors' intentions to create financial returns and a social or environmental impact captured in the evaluation and selection of impact investing opportunities?
- What is the appropriate operating framework for evaluating impact investing options?
- Given the broad universe of potential impact investments, how

can impact investors most efficiently and effectively make these investment decisions?

- How can investments be made at sufficient financial scale without diluting the impact?
- How can organizations develop an impact investing policy to address strategic and governance issues?
- What are the organizational changes needed to implement impact investing and how can impact investors select the right advisors and partners?
- What are the appropriate legal structures for impact investing vehicles?
- How can impact investors evaluate the trade-off between a focus on specific impact themes and the need to apply portfolio diversification and asset allocation tools most effectively?
- How can impact investors integrate aspects of behavioral finance?

To provide a framework in which impact investors can move toward action, we separate impact investing into two distinct activities:
(1) Establishing an Impact Investing Strategy; and
(2) Implementing and Maintaining an Impact Investing Strategy.

The Impact Investing Cycle

Establish Strategy				Implement and Maintain Strategy		
Articulate Mission and Values	Create Impact Themes	Define Impact	Develop Impact Investing Policy	Generate Deal Flow	Analyze Deals	Evaluate Impact

We first outline how an impact investor can develop a strategy and then translate that strategy into concrete implementation steps. In this split between strategy and execution, we see the Impact Investing Policy as the critical link. The Impact Investing Policy is the tangible result of establishing an Impact Investing Strategy. It explicitly articulates hypotheses, or theories of change, about how the investment will generate a social and/or environmental impact. To date, these assumptions have not typically been rigorously defined, and investors have relied on loose theories of change in order to support their investments. Most impact investors have expended considerable effort in developing and articulating their mission and are now focusing on the execution steps of generating deal flow, analyzing deals and monitoring. However, the initial analysis or investment thesis about how a specific investment will create impact remains underdeveloped. We also draw upon developments in asset allocation and behavioral finance to provide deeper insight into the impact investing theses in specific sectors and to serve as tools for assisting impact investors in making prudent investment decisions. All of these steps continuously inform the Impact Investing Policy and often result in adjustments to and adaptations of portions of the Impact Investing Policy including asset allocation, definition and evaluation of impact.

To help illustrate these concepts, we have selected the following three organizations for their work in impact investing across missions, values, impact themes and levels of engagement. They act as direct investors, make investments through third parties, and in the case of RSF Social Finance and the Calvert Foundation, structure products for other impact investors.

- **RSF Social Finance** (www.rsfsocialfinance.org) is a 501(c)(3) public foundation originally established in 1936 to support projects inspired by the work of social philosopher Rudolf Steiner. Today, RSF's mission is to transform the way the world works with money by providing innovative investing, lending and giving services that address key issues in the areas of Food & Agriculture, Education & the Arts, and Ecological Stewardship.

- **The KL Felicitas Foundation** (www.klfelicitasfoundation.org), a California-based private family foundation, was established by the Kleissner family in 2000 with the following mission: to enable social entrepreneurs and enterprises worldwide to grow sustainably, with an emphasis on rural communities and families; and advocate the foundation's sustainability, mission, and social investment strategy.

- **The Calvert Social Investment Foundation** (www.calvertfoundation.org), a 501(c)3 non-profit corporation, was launched in 1988 with the support of the socially responsible mutual fund company, Calvert Group Ltd. and several major foundations. Calvert Foundation's mission is to maximize the flow of capital to disadvantaged communities in order to foster a more equitable and sustainable society. Calvert Foundation's goal is to end poverty through investment.

Harnessing the Genius of AND

Today, the field of impact investing has all of the necessary pieces in place for investors to create and execute innovative solutions to address critical social and environmental issues. The intent of this monograph is to provide an effective and persuasive toolkit that pulls together all of these financial and non-financial pieces. Impact Investors are successfully harnessing the Genius of AND to effect real change across impact themes ranging from community-based water projects in the developing world to improving education in the US. We hope to inspire you to roll up your sleeves and take on the hard but rewarding work of impact investing and make its promise a reality.

1 www.blendedvalue.org

2 "McKinsey's Approach to Learning for Social Impact," Discussion Paper, Draft June 2009.

3 Freireich, Jessica and Katherine Fulton, "Investing for Social & Environmental Impact," Monitor Institute, 2009.

4 Collins, James C. and Jerry I. Porras, "Built to Last: Successful Habits of Visionary Companies," 1997.

Chapter 2:

Articulating Mission and Values

Establish Strategy				Implement and Maintain Strategy		
Articulate Mission and Values	Create Impact Themes	Define Impact	Develop Impact Investing Policy	Generate Deal Flow	Analyze Deals	Evaluate Impact

The Road Map

Your impact investing strategy should be firmly aligned with your personal or institution's core values and mission. Reflecting Rockefeller Philanthropy Advisors' own mission of helping donors create thoughtful, effective philanthropy throughout the world, the following questions were developed as a Philanthropic Road Map to assist donors in structuring their goals and missions. We have adapted this Philanthropic Road Map to become the Impact Investing Roadmap. This tool can help you clarify your motivations, select impact themes, determine your approach to these issues and structure your actions. Consider the following questions as a way to determine your current position and clarify assumptions before formalizing an impact investing strategy.

*Motivation: **Why are you interested in impact investing?*** Some answers include: seeking an enhanced financial return while making positive social and/or environmental impacts; heritage; expression of values; leaving a legacy; affiliations; causes; involving younger generations; environmental awareness; social change; making a difference; giving back; creating a vehicle for working with your family; exploring your interests; using your talents and skills for a different purpose; supporting the people and institutions important to you.

Issues: What issues will your impact investing address? Do you want to address widespread global problems such as poverty, disease or climate change, or would you rather focus on specific or domestic issues like literacy, local education or affordable housing? Geographic choices must also be made as well as decisions about how you can best effect change — through leaders, institutions or both?

Approaches: The How and When of Your Theory of Change. What is your strategy to make this change happen? Is it through policy, advocacy, research, grassroots or a national versus local campaign? What problem are you trying to solve and how do you solve it? What organizations, institutions and partners should be involved? Where are the gaps? Do you want to support philanthropic efforts or attract commercial capital? How will you assess progress? How will you implement the strategy?

Involvement: The Who. How would you like to be involved in and manage your impact investing? Hands-on management, formal or informal management structures, collaborative or independent?

*Evaluation: **What is your time horizon and level of engagement?*** What is your tolerance for risk? How do you define success or progress toward your goal?

The complete Impact Investing Road Map should identify your motivations and issues, define your goals and approaches for key issues, and select the appropriate types of investments. It will become part of your Impact Investing Policy. Based on this Road Map, you will be in a position to see and assess results, and adjust as needed. Your mission and values can then be operationalized through the appropriate legal structures and investment vehicles.

Applying the Road Map/Articulating the Mission

We first present how RSF Social Finance, the KL Felicitas Foundation and The Calvert Social Investment Foundation developed their missions, created their impact investing philosophies and identified their impact investing themes. We also note how they approach financial first and impact first transactions and select their partners and advisors. We then highlight how they have translated their strategies into concrete impact themes in order to reflect their theories of change. And finally, we share how they are applying tools such as asset allocation and portfolio theory to deal generation, due diligence, portfolio monitoring and a customized evaluation process to fine tune their strategies over time.

RSF Social Finance

RSF Social Finance (RSF) was incorporated in 1936 and until 1983 engaged exclusively in fundraising and charitable giving to organizations inspired by the work of Austrian social philosopher Rudolf Steiner. In 1984, RSF began providing direct loans to organizations that likewise supported Steiner's insights on associative economics and social renewal. Then, in the late 1990s, RSF expanded its mission to serve a broader range of clients with compatible values and intentions, including those engaged in non-profit and for-profit social enterprise. Today, RSF offers investing, lending and philanthropic services. RSF strives to create innovative financial vehicles that not only generate deep social and environmental impact, but also foster community among participants. RSF currently has more than 1,000 clients and $130 million in consolidated assets, and has made over $190 million in loans and over $90 million in grants since 1984.

RSF frames all of its work in terms of an overarching purpose to transform the way the world works with money. This purpose is informed by the following set of core values:

Spirit: The primary role of money is to serve the highest intentions of the human spirit.

Trust: People are best served by financial transactions that are direct, transparent and personal, based on long-term relationships.

Interdependence: Economic success will be defined by social and ecological impact, not by financial results alone.

Community: Networks and associations will be increasingly important in the circulation of money.

Innovation: A deeply entrepreneurial culture is required to generate breakthrough ideas at the intersection of social change and finance.

Equality: All those seeking to align their values and their money will have access to opportunities for investing, lending and giving.

With regard to impact investing, RSF offers funds designed to serve a range of individual and institutional investors. The funds include a core lending program of short-term notes supporting non-profit and for-profit social enterprises; a mezzanine debt fund providing growth capital for for-profit social enterprises; and a program-related investment (PRI) fund designed for foundations wishing to invest in PRIs but lacking the in-house capacity to do so.

KL Felicitas Foundation

The KL Felicitas Foundation (KL Felicitas) founders, Charly and Lisa Kleissner, first became interested in sustainability, mission and social investments as a way to break down the "value/ethic firewall" between their personal and business lives. Impact investing is a logical extension of their core beliefs. It enables the foundation to use a wide range of investment vehicles to support social enterprises, including grants, social loans, loan guarantees and private equity. Impact investing also allows family foundations like KL Felicitas with assets of approximately $10 million to maximize their impact by augmenting annual grantmaking with the effects of an investment strategy aligned with their mission. The Kleissners apply the following approach/values to their personal lives and work including their role as trustees of the foundation:

- Commitment to high touch;
- Belief that a grass-roots approach is more successful and sustainable than a top-down approach;
- Belief that systemic societal problems can be addressed most effectively through cross-sector partnerships, market forces and/or hybrid solutions;
- Commitment to leverage as many aspects of the foundation's structure and activities as possible; and
- Commitment to considering the holistic impact of everything they do.

Calvert Social Investment Foundation

The Calvert Social Investment Foundation (Calvert Foundation) was launched in 1988 with the mission of maximizing the flow of capital to disadvantaged communities. Although it was launched with the support of Calvert Group, Ltd., and major national foundations, Calvert Foundation operates as an autonomous non-profit entity. Calvert Foundation's investment philosophy is to provide investors a modest financial return while generating a high social impact. The foundation is able to provide needed capital to underserved markets while seeking to control risk for investors. Calvert Foundation places loans primarily with affordable housing lenders and developers, small business lenders, microfinance institutions and other community development organizations that have a track record of success. Calvert Foundation operates three main programs:

Community Investment Notes:
Calvert Foundation issues Community Investment Notes (Notes), which are senior, general recourse obligations of the

foundation paying investors a below-market fixed interest rate. Investors accept this below-market interest rate in exchange for supporting the positive social impact generated by Notes proceeds. These proceeds are invested in a diversified pool of high credit-quality non-profit financial intermediaries, federally-insured community development banks and credit unions, affordable housing developers, marketable fixed income securities, microfinance institutions, fair trade cooperatives, and for-profit social enterprises. As of year-end 2008, Notes sales exceeded $158 million to more than 4,600 investors.

Community Investment Partners:
Community Investment Partners (CIP), Calvert Foundation's business services unit, offers consulting, analysis, asset management and capital markets solutions to institutional and individual investors who wish to create or enhance their community investment programs, and to organizations wanting to raise capital through non-traditional distribution networks. At year-end 2008, CIP was servicing 26 clients, representing an additional $66 million in community investment assets under management.

Calvert Giving Fund:
The Calvert Giving Fund, Calvert Foundation's socially responsible donor-advised fund, provides donors opportunities to: make tax-deductible donations to the Giving Fund; invest their donated assets in the Calvert Group socially-screened mutual fund Notes, or alternative socially responsible instruments; and recommend donations to non-profit organizations around the world. Calvert Giving Fund was launched in 2000, and at year-end 2008 had net assets of over $26 million from 413 donor-advisors.

Impact First, Financial First and Blended Transactions

As demonstrated by RSF, KL Felicitas and Calvert Foundation, impact investors can have distinct approaches to the question of financial return and impact. Calvert and RFS offer impact first only investments to their clients. KL Felicitas utilizes all three types of investments in their portfolio — impact first, financial first and blended transactions.

In some circumstances, investors with different return requirements will co-invest in the same enterprise or project. In these collaborative deals, it makes sense for the financial first and impact first investors to combine capital to fund the transaction. This type of structure is also widely used by the public sector to attract capital into particular target programs or industries (e.g., the US Federal Government's Low Income Housing Tax Credit or the International Finance Corporation's risk-sharing structures with private investors). In these structures, the impact first investors must be very clear as to how their subsidy of financial first investors is increasing the overall impact and capital of the project and not just de-risking the deal for the commercial investors.

KL Felicitas supports the view that many systemic approaches to social issues require a partial subsidy in the form of a grant or a PRI. In these deals, the partial subsidy often reduces the risk for the financial first investment in a partner organization. These types of hybrid investments should ideally achieve an impact that could not otherwise be accomplished.

Chapter 3:

Creating Impact Themes

Establish Strategy

| Articulate Mission and Values | Create Impact Themes | Define Impact | Develop Impact Investing Policy |

Implement and Maintain Strategy

| Generate Deal Flow | Analyze Deals | Evaluate Impact |

Impact Investment Theme Selection

Once your organization has defined its mission and target areas of impact, you will face the challenge of translating impact themes into investment themes. At first glance, this appears to be a simple exercise, but it may ultimately require significant time and research. The gears of impact and investment opportunity must be tightly aligned if your impact investments are to be successful. Our team has reviewed the universe of possible social, environmental and blended impact themes investors and fund managers might pursue. In many instances, funds aim for social and/or environmental impact in more than one of these areas. This is by no means a comprehensive list, but some of the more common themes which we have found impact investors organized around include:

• Climate Change;

• Energy;

• Water;

- Community Development;
- Social Enterprises;
- Health & Wellness;
- Sustainable Development; and
- Education.

The impact themes RSF, KL Felicitas and Calvert Foundation have used to define their impact investment activities provide insight into how impact investors are translating impact goals into investment themes. Even among these impact investors, there is a clear diversity of impact themes. The integration of impact themes across investment asset classes is presented in Chapter 5.

RSF Social Finance:

RSF's impact themes are derived from its three impact focus areas: Food & Agriculture; Education & the Arts; and Ecological Stewardship. Food & Agriculture supports diversification, region-first approaches and sustainable practices. Education & the Arts invests in initiatives that address the intellectual, emotional, aesthetic and social needs of children and adults. Fine arts and performing arts include investments that foster spiritual awareness or increase access to learning and the arts for all communities; entrepreneurship, job training, consumer education and other awareness-building programs; and handicrafts produced and distributed according to fair trade principles. Ecological Stewardship promotes energy- and eco-efficiency; green building materials and green consumer products; ecological remediation and restoration, land conservation and land trusts; and environmental legal defense.

KL Felicitas Foundation:

KL Felicitas Foundation's mission is to enable social entrepreneurs and enterprises worldwide to grow sustainably, with an emphasis on rural communities and families. These social enterprises can be for-profit ventures, non-profit ventures, or hybrid ventures that combine the passion and aspiration of a social/environmental mission with the discipline, innovation and determination commonly associated with a for-profit business. These social enterprises should have one or more of the following characteristics: (1) they provide goods and services for the poor or disadvantaged, and/or (2) they employ people from the poor or disadvantaged, and/or (3) they are majority owned by the poor or disadvantaged communities. KL Felicitas's definition of social enterprise is broad and not limited to particular impact themes like healthcare, education or water. Therefore, its investments are spread across a range of impact themes.

Calvert Foundation:

Calvert Foundation seeks to use investment as a tool to end poverty. Calvert Foundation's capital is placed with local intermediaries who enable individuals, families and whole communities to work their way out of poverty. In the US, Calvert Foundation finances community development financial institutions, affordable housing developers and other local social enterprises. Overseas, the foundation reaches microfinance institutions, fair-trade cooperatives and other community development initiatives.

Selecting the Right Partners and Advisors

Building the right team to execute an impact investing strategy is critical to your success. While other sectors of investment management such as tax, legal and portfolio management have become increasingly specialized, you may find that impact investing falls between the insulated fields of philanthropy and investment. Several barriers exist for the efficient delivery of impact investment advisory services:

- Impact investing requires active ownership, and there are typically several layers of intermediaries between the asset owner (donor, trustee, individual, institution) and the ultimate deployment of the capital;
- Disconnect between long-term investment objective of impact investors and investment consultants who are evaluated on a short-term basis;
- Lack of consensus on how to define and measure social and environmental impact with most consultants either using a "you-know-it-when-you-see-it" approach, or deferring judgment on social and environmental issues to their clients;
- Advisors typically focus on select assets rather than offering services across all asset classes;
- Lack of existing investment infrastructure means significant cost associated with research and due diligence of impact investments, particularly for international strategies; and
- Lack of consensus and/or understanding between investor and advisors on impact thesis.

At present, the relationship between impact investors and their financial advisors follows two distinct models:

- The financial advisor may also be the impact investment advisor; or

- Impact analysis is provided separately by a specialist and must be coordinated with traditional financial advisors' workflows.

Despite these challenges, new service providers have emerged to provide solutions due to the pioneering efforts of impact investors throughout the field. These new service providers include institutional consulting firms, global asset management firms, private banks, specialized product providers, boutique advisory practices and thematic research providers along with peer networking and collaborative investor groups of impact investors. These impact advisory service providers are helping to break down the barriers and build the field of impact investing.

Impact Investor Resources:

Investors should also seek out resources and networks created for impact investors which focus on specific impact themes and investment vehicles.

Impact Investor Resources:
- Blended Value (www.blendedvalue.org)
- Boston College Institute for Responsible Investment (www.bcccc.net)
- Carbon Disclosure Project (www.cdproject.net)
- Certified B Corporation (www.bcorporation.net)
- Charity SRI (www.charitysri.org)
- CleanTech Venture Network (www.cleantechnetwork.com)
- ClearlySo (www.clearlyso.com)
- Community Development Bankers Association (www.communitydevelopmentbanks.org)
- Community Development Venture Capital Alliance (www.cdvca.org)
- Community Investing Center Database (www.communityinvestingcenterdb.org)
- Confluence Philanthropy (www.confluencephilanthropy.org)
- Corporate Impact Reporting (www.iosreporting.org)

continued

- Environmental Defense Fund Innovation Exchange (www.innovation.edf.org/home.cfm)
- Global Impact Investing Network (www.globalimpactinvestingnetwork.org)
- GreenBiz.com (www.greenbiz.com)
- Greentech Media (www.greentechmedia.com)
- Impact Reporting and Investment Standards (www.iris-standards.org)
- Initiative for a Competitive Inner City (www.icic.org)
- Institutional Investors Group on Climate Change (www.iigcc.org)
- International Association of Microfinance Investors (www.iamfi.com)
- Investors Circle (www.investorscircle.net)
- Microcapital (www.microcapital.org)
- MIX Market Microfinance Information Platform (www.mixmarket.org)
- More for Mission – The Campaign for Mission Investing (www.moreformission.org)
- New Economics Foundation (www.neweconomics.org)
- New Energy Finance (www.newenergyfinance.com)
- NextBillion.net (www.nextbillion.net)
- PRI Makers Network (www.primakers.net)
- Principles for Responsible Investment (www.unpri.org)
- Research Initiative on Social Entrepreneurship (www.riseproject.org)
- Responsible Investor (www.responsible-investor.com)
- Responsible Property Initiative (responsibleproperty.net)
- Rockefeller Philanthropy Advisors (www.rockpa.org);
- Social Enterprise Innovation Network (www.sein.net)
- Social Finance (www.socialfinance.org.uk)
- Social Funds (www.socialfunds.com)
- Social Investment Forum (www.socialinvest.org)
- Social ROI: A Social Entrepreneurship Blog (www.socialroi.com)
- Social Venture Network (www.svn.org)
- Stanford Social Innovation Review (www.ssireview.org)
- Symbiotics (www.symbiotics.ch)
- The Nature Conservancy (www.nature.org)
- The UNEP Finance Initiative Asset Management Working Group (www.unepfi.org)
- Triplepundit (www.triplepundit.com)
- Xigi.net (www.xigi.net)

Chapter 4:

Defining Impact

Establish Strategy				Implement and Maintain Strategy		
Articulate Mission and Values	Create Impact Themes	Define Impact	Develop Impact Investing Policy	Generate Deal Flow	Analyze Deals	Evaluate Impact

Impact investors generally make assumptions about how their investments can translate into desired social or environmental impacts. Some of these assumptions are explicit in terms of outputs while others are implicit. These impact investment theses are also known as theories of change and describe the step-by-step process through which a particular investment activity will translate into a desired outcome. In *Philanthropy's New Passing Gear: Mission-Related Investing*, we defined five distinct tools impact investors can use. Each has its own impact investment thesis. The first tools of active ownership strategies and screening are values-based tactics. The other three — financial first investments, impact first investments and guarantees — have specific social and environmental impacts and represent the majority of the impact investing we will outline in this monograph. For each of the tools, we have included the related impact investment thesis or theory of change.

Impact Investing Tools & Tactics

Active Ownership Strategies

As a long-term owner and fiduciary of holdings in publicly-traded securities, you have the ability to influence corporate behavior and further your desired impact through proxy voting, shareholder resolutions and informal shareholder engagement with the corporate management of the companies you hold in your portfolio. Many companies have changed their policies and practices on a host of issues important to impact investors, not only because of market forces, but also because their shareholders demanded change.

Impact Investment Thesis: Constructively engaging with the management of publicly-traded companies through proxy voting, shareholder resolutions and engagement will cause companies to stop undesired activities or begin desired activities of importance to a specific impact investor and to the company's array of stakeholders.

Screening

Screening is the practice of buying and selling publicly-traded securities based on the evaluation of impact criteria that reflect your personal or institution's values. Your investment decision may be to avoid certain companies (negative screening) or to support particular companies (positive or best-in-class screening). The ultimate goal of screening is for your portfolio to reflect your values and mission, mitigate risks and use your investment capital to encourage or discourage specific corporate behaviors.[5]

Impact Investment Thesis: The buying and/or selling of a publicly-traded security will cause companies to stop undesired activities or start desired activities.

Active Ownership Strategies and Screening can also create market signals about the specific companies and set the terms for public debate of corporate behaviors. These tactics can be accomplished at low cost and may be fully leveraged by partnering with other investor groups.

Impact First Investments

Impact first investments can be made by foundations as well as public sector and high net-worth impact investors. Some impact investments made by US foundation impact investors are categorized as program-related investments (PRIs).[6]

Impact Investment Thesis: The investment will directly generate specific desired outcomes (e.g., units of housing created, land preserved or children immunized). The subsidy enables an additional outcome that would otherwise not be possible.

Financial First Investments

Financial first investments create a risk-adjusted rate of return in addition to creating specific desired outcomes. For example, public and private pension funds, along with insurance companies and other institutional investors, are increasingly seeking to attract capital to underserved urban markets and build assets in low-income communities. These programs target financial first returns against established financial benchmarks in addition to generating social and environmental benefits.

Impact Investment Thesis: The investment will generate specific desired outcomes similar to impact first, but without subsidy.

Guarantees

Guarantees are another important tool impact investors use to mitigate the credit risk created by an organization when it receives a loan from a bank or other lending institution. You can use your assets as collateral to provide security (guarantee) to an organization based on this collateral. Unlike other impact investments, a guarantee may not require upfront deployment of cash by the impact investor. Through guarantees, an investor can create more impact by leveraging his guarantee with additional capital from other investors. For example, a recent partnership between the Nairobi-based Alliance for a Green Revolution and South African-based Standard Bank exemplifies the power of guarantees. By committing $10 million to cover potential losses in a targeted loan portfolio, the Alliance induced Standard Bank to commit $100 million in loans to farmers in Africa who would otherwise be unable to access finance.

Impact Investment Thesis: The investment will generate specific desired impacts and additional leverage.

Articulating An Impact Investment Thesis

As the industry of impact investing coalesces, and global investors begin to organize and coordinate more effectively, standard frameworks for structuring and articulating an impact investment thesis are developing. In the meantime, pioneers in the field have developed their own approaches to articulating impact investment theses. These tend to remain quite subjective and specific to the context of the investor's motivations. However, they provide structures that other investors can draw on in developing their own approach. For example, RSF Social

Finance has developed distinct impact criteria for evaluating potential loans through its Core Lending program:

Core Lending Impact Criteria
- Product — generates major shift in consumer preferences.
- Manufacturing processes — utilizes sustainable energy use, waste management, etc.
- Supply chain — seeks highest values alignment possible.
- Employee practices — strives for high positive impact; includes profit/ownership sharing.
- Community — maintains strong presence beyond token contributions.
- Governance Structure — allows entrepreneurs' values to stay intact.
- The entrepreneur is committed to changing the rules and practices of an entire industry.

For Calvert Foundation's Community Investment Note, potential borrowers must have an explicit focus on serving low-income communities and individuals, or on providing financial services to individuals without access to traditional sources of capital. Borrowers must be engaged in community development initiatives that help expand opportunities, promote job growth, develop small business and promote homeownership in underserved areas. The foundation lends to organizations that work in both urban and rural settings, in the US and abroad.

The Calvert Foundation's Global Impact Ventures (GIV) funds allow donor advisors to invest in funds that have private debt and/or equity stakes in social enterprises, innovative non-profits and microfinance institutions. Many of them provide unique "gap-filling" financing — channeling capital to markets that cannot get financing from traditional commercial sources.

This funding helps organizations scale, and in many instances allows them to develop their business models to the point where more traditional financing becomes available to them.

Evolution To More Direct Impact

RSF's donor-advised fund offering has evolved over time to create opportunities for more direct impact investments. Prior to 2004, RSF provided interest rate returns to donor-advised

Meyer Memorial Trust's Geographic Impact Thesis

Meyer Memorial Trust (MMT) was created by the late Fred G. Meyer who built the chain of retail stores bearing his name throughout the Pacific Northwest. MMT is a private, independent foundation with the stated mission "to invest in people, ideas and efforts that deliver significant social benefit to Oregon and southwest Washington." MMT operates three programs: Strategic Initiatives, Grants and Program-Related Investments. MMT has developed and documented an effective means to prioritize its impact investing opportunities. As illustrated at right, MMT uses a multi-tiered geographic model to define its impact thesis. MMT adopted this model in 2008 and applies it to their investment analysis as they expand their impact investment portfolio. MMT prioritizes investments having direct environmental, social or economic impact (ES&I) within the state of Oregon, the MMT's service region. MMT then recognizes the ES&I impact benefits that investments may offer the Pacific Northwest and beyond. MMT gives lower priority to investments creating no impact (benefit or harm) in its stated mission areas. Finally, MMT seeks to understand, avoid and over time eliminate any investments deemed to directly harm or operate in a manner contrary to the MMT's mission.

funds based on RSF's cost of capital, as is typical for many non-profit intermediaries. Beginning in 2004, RSF designed a traditional socially-responsible investment (SRI) program (i.e., screening and active ownership strategies) by contracting with several SRI asset managers within three portfolios — Equity, Fixed Income and Cash. Investments were primarily in public equity, public debt and cash, making it difficult to determine the degree to which investments were aligned with RSF's mission and theory of change. In 2005, RSF moved to a more directly managed SRI program with one institution providing expertise

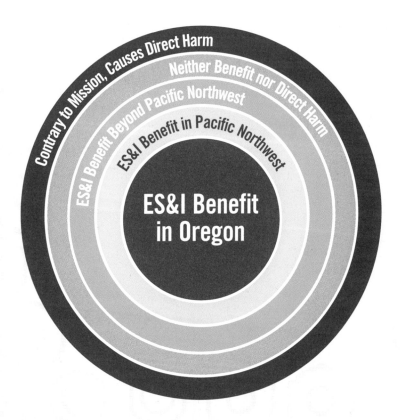

E = Environmental   S = Social   I = Economic Impact   *Source: Meyer Memorial Trust*

in the field of screening, advocacy and solutions-based impact investing. Nevertheless, as investments were still primarily in public equity, public debt and cash, it remained difficult to determine the impact being generated.

Following a strategic review in 2007, RSF designed and implemented a more direct and transparent donor-advised fund investment program in order to achieve the deepest possible social impact through these investments. As part of this new program, RSF expanded its holdings in private equity and private debt vehicles, and modified its due diligence process to include more extensive analysis of potential investees' social impact. Donor-advised fund accounts are now invested in three portfolios called Impact, Liquidity and Transformation, all of which aim to reduce unnecessary levels of intermediation while continuing to meet rigorous diversification, risk and return criteria. Within the Liquidity Portfolio, for example, RSF has begun the process of transferring all money market and commercial paper investments into deposits at the highest-performing community development and environmental banks in the country. Within the Impact Portfolio, RSF invested in Beartooth Capital, a private real estate fund that generates strong financial returns through the restoration and protection of ecologically important ranch land. (See Case Study in Chapter 8.) This investment contributed both to RSF's goal of making more direct investments as well as diversifying the portfolio through the addition of real assets. Going even further toward direct investing, the Transformation portfolio is designed to make direct venture and debt investments in enterprises that seek to solve the most pressing social and environmental issues of core importance to RSF and its clients. RSF believes that by pursuing more direct investment opportunities, it will be better able to ensure mission alignment and report on the concrete social and environmental impacts of its investments.

KL Felicitas Foundation

KL Felicitas initially used negative screening as its impact investing strategy, but soon realized that the impact was indirect, unleveraged and unaligned as well as nearly impossible to measure. At the same time, they made the strategic decision to hire a team of advisors rather than rely on any one consultant or firm to provide full services. This approach brought together the best possible team from multiple disciplines (e.g., family coach, family office manager, tax advisor, philanthropic advisor and investment advisor). In addition to providing the desired 'checks and balances,' this approach fosters high engagement by all team members.

The Kleissners began to explore philanthropy more deeply and were introduced to Jed Emerson's thoughts on blended value investments. Participation in The Philanthropy Workshop West (www.tpwwest.org) and the Global Philanthropy Forum (www.philanthropyforum.org) further exposed them to international investment and grant opportunities. A key turning point in the process occurred when the foundation merged its impact investing policy with its asset allocation strategy and formalized the deal flow process. KL Felicitas organizes its impact investing activities into four categories: Sustainability Investments, Mission-Related Investments, Program-Related Investments and Social Component Investments. It is important to point out that the Kleissners are not only engaged in impact investing in their family foundation, but are actively doing impact investing with the assets of their Family Limited Partnerships and Charitable Remainder Trusts as well.

KL Felicitas believes that helping social entrepreneurs and social enterprises reach scale in a more sustainable and impactful way can make a meaningful contribution to the alleviation of poverty, as these social enterprises either provide affordable goods and services or meaningful employment for the poor and disadvantaged.

In addition to Program-Related Investments and Mission-Related Investments, KL Felicitas also uses 'Sustainability Investments' and 'Social Component Investments' as part of its overall impact investment strategy. The foundation has set an aggressive goal to move to 100% impact investments. Since it will take time to find appropriate Mission- and Program-Related Investments for all its assets, KL Felicitas decided to invest and track 'Sustainability Investments' and 'Social Component Investments' (aligned with their values, but not with their mission or programs) while moving into more Mission- and Program-Related Investments.

KL Felicitas defines Social Component Investments as investments that allocate part of their profits either directly or indirectly to social beneficiaries. Since these types of investments are not directly aligned with KL Felicitas' mission, opportunities in this space are evaluated opportunistically. Given a choice between a Non-Social Component Investment and a Social Component Investment in the same asset class, KL Felicitas Foundation chooses the latter.

KL Felicitas defines Sustainability Investment as investments having a demonstrable focus on holistic sustainability, i.e., sustainability from an economic, environmental, social and spiritual perspective. KL Felicitas does not yet have a core set of simple and easily understood indicators and metrics to demonstrate this type of holistic sustainability, so it is using a set of discrete sustainability indicators in its due diligence process as described on its website.

Chapter 4: Defining Impact

Beyond Rational Man: Incorporating Behavioral Finance into Impact Investing

As impact investors seek to more tightly link investment and impact, behavioral finance can be a powerful tool to better define their impact investment thesis. Traditional finance uses models in which the economic agents are assumed to be rational. While this framework is appealingly simple, it has become clear that basic facts about markets are not easily understood within this framework. Behavioral finance is based on the alternative notion that most investors are subject to behavioral biases that can cause their financial decisions to be less than fully rational.[7] Validated through empirical research and experimentation, behavioral finance is increasingly recognized for its power to explain human and investment behavior more accurately than traditional models.

Altruism, psychologically induced mistakes, externalities and information asymmetries all create opportunities for impact investors to make a difference. For example, information asymmetries can lead to capital gaps in underserved urban and rural areas creating opportunities overlooked by conventional investors. Climate change is arguably the most important externality facing the global community. The failure of the global community to act quickly in order to fashion a collective response has a significant psychological component. In the past, altruism led some people to expend their own resources in an effort to address climate change through research and the sharing of information.

Impact investors, with the appropriate knowledge, experience and inclination, also have a role to play in developing systems and social infrastructure. This type of investment can focus on building people's skills with the goal of helping communities become self-sufficient. We know from experience that both governments and markets can fail, and some of those failures present opportunities for impact investors. Altruism and narrow self-interest co-exist in most people. For most people there are limits to how much they are willing to sacrifice in order to help others. Some impact investors are willing to accept lower financial returns relative to risk in exchange for generating a social benefit, or what some might call a social return. Others are willing to engage in impact investing, as long as they do not need to sacrifice financial returns while pursuing impact objectives.

Behavioral finance has several implications when it comes to impact investing. First, impact investing adds value when it is able to counter some form of market failure. Second, investors will benefit if they understand the psychology which underlies a market failure. Third, the activity of impact investing will increase if investors become more comfortable with it. In his book *The Management Illusion*, Hersh Shefrin developed a checklist for managers to test whether they are subject to behavioral biases. This checklist is also useful for assessing impact investment opportunities. Below you will find examples of these behavioral biases. Each example is presented in three parts: a definition; diagnostic questions; and an illustration of the concept.

1. Overconfidence — Investors overestimate their ability and the accuracy of the information they have.
- *Are we as good as we think we are? Are we too sure of our views? Are we underestimating risks?*

In a recent article in *The New Yorker*, Malcolm Gladwell places the responsibility for a large part of the current financial crisis on the systemic overconfidence of investors — particularly the senior managers of large Wall Street investment banks such as Bear Stearns.[8]

2. Unrealistic Optimism — Individuals attach too high a probability to events favorable to them, and too low a probability to events unfavorable to them.
• *Are we looking at the world through rose-colored glasses?*

3. Representativeness — Investors place excessive reliance on stereotypes, for example by equating good stocks with good companies.
• *In making judgments, are we placing too much reliance on stereotypes?*

This bias is particularly relevant for impact investors who often are seeking to fill gaps created by the lack of information in specific impact themes such as the financial performance of charter schools or the repayment rates of microfinance borrowers.

4. Conservatism — Forecasters cling to prior beliefs in the face of new information.
• *Are we downplaying information we don't want to hear, and playing up information that we do want to hear?*

Despite substantial initial public offerings of stock and mergers and acquisitions in India, many investors still hesitate from making impact equity investments in social enterprises in India due to their incorrect belief that exit strategies do not exist.

5. Availability Bias/Recency Effect — Investors overweigh readily-available information, e.g., by overstating recently observed events.

* *Are we placing too much weight on evidence that is in front of us, or easily recalled, and insufficient weight on information that is harder to obtain, or less easily recalled?*

Impact investors investing in alternative asset classes sometimes only review a very small slice of data to make their investment choices. Since it may be impossible for them to view and analyze the rest of the data, they may base their decision on this readily-available data only instead of completing the appropriate due diligence process.

6. Framing and Anchoring — The form of presentation of information can affect the decision made. When the presentation of information is clear, the frame is said to be transparent. Otherwise the frame is said to be opaque.

* *Are we using judgments that start with an anchor from which we make adjustments? If so, are we adjusting enough?*

Many impact investing opportunities — particularly in developing countries — might not yet have public relations expertise to present themselves in the way expected by investors in developed countries. This might lead to a decision not to invest, even though the underlying fundamentals are good. Conversely, fledgling social enterprises effectively utilizing modern media tools might be able to present an overly optimistic picture. Both of these examples accentuate the need for solid due diligence.

7. Mental Accounting — Individuals allocate wealth to separate mental compartments and ignore fungibility and correlation effects.

As outlined throughout this monograph, impact investing reflects the desire by investors to overcome the bias that financial assets dedicated to financial return cannot be mixed with assets targeted toward the creation of social or environmental impact. This is particularly true in private foundations with sharp separation of their endowment investment and grantmaking activities.

8. Regret and Loss Aversion, and Aversion to a Sure Loss — Individuals make decisions in a way that allows them to avoid feeling emotional pain in the event of an adverse outcome. Individuals can be too conservative, because they are extremely sensitive to the pain of loss.

- *When things don't turn out as we expected, are we prone to feel regret, meaning the pain from imagining ourselves to have made a different decision?*
- *Are we prone to make decisions with a view toward minimizing anticipated regret?*
- *At the same time, might our attitudes toward bearing risk change dramatically if we view ourselves as facing the possibility of having to accept a loss?*
- *Are we reluctant to accept losses, instead taking chances where we have to beat the odds in order to be successful?*

Many investors might shy away from impact investments in general or from impact investments in early stage social enterprises not only because of the risk associated with these types of investments, but because of the fear of an adverse investment outcome.

Market Failures and Impact Investing

Impact investors have positive roles to play in addressing market failures, especially when it comes to dealing with issues involving public goods, externalities, and imperfect information. In this regard, consider the upcoming case studies in this volume:

- **Triodos Sustainable Trade Fund** — a guarantee fund that allows investors to support trade financing for certified fair trade and organic producers, and

- **Dial 1298 for Ambulance** — a for-profit social enterprise providing emergency medical service ambulances in India.

Water and energy tend to be natural monopolies while health and education are public goods. Environmental sustainability falls into the category of externalities. But what about ambulance services, especially if the intended market consists of low income households unable to pay? As we shall see in the description of the case, the business model to address this issue involves the ability to engage in cross subsidization, thereby exploiting a market failure for this purpose.

We see a clear role for behavioral finance in impact investing, particularly in how aspects of behavioral finance can help investors articulate and better frame their impact investment theses. In some cases, impact investing can even be viewed as correcting behavioral finance biases, which traditional market mechanisms are not addressing. By being cognizant of our biases, and on the look-out for potential market failures, the impact investor can invest both more prudently and create more positive social and environmental impact.

5 Investors should be aware that screened portfolio performance may or may not have the same performance as an unscreened portfolio when measured against a selected benchmark. Screening out certain companies also makes it impossible to take active ownership positions. Studies about the relationship between screening and investment performance are available at www.sristudies.org.

6 PRIs can be in the form of debt or equity and must be made with the primary intent to further program objectives. Following are the three criteria in the Tax Reform Act of 1969 section 4944 — used by the IRS to determine if an investment can be categorized as a PRI: The primary purpose of the investment is to advance the foundation's charitable objectives; neither the production of income nor appreciation of property is the primary purpose; and the funds cannot be used directly or indirectly to lobby for political purposes.

7 See Krugman, Paul, "How Did Economists Get It So Wrong?," *New York Times*, September 6, 2009 for a discussion of behavioral finance's role in the financial crisis.

8 Gladwell, Malcolm, "Cocksure: Banks, Battles, and the Psychology of Overconfidence," *The New Yorker*, July 29, 2009.

Chapter 5:
Developing an Impact Investing Policy

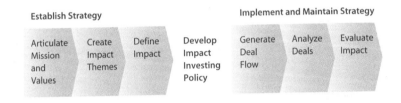

Establish Strategy | Implement and Maintain Strategy

Articulate Mission and Values → Create Impact Themes → Define Impact → Develop Impact Investing Policy → Generate Deal Flow → Analyze Deals → Evaluate Impact

Once you decide to proceed with an impact investment strategy and have articulated an impact thesis, the process of translating this effort into a working portfolio begins. As outlined in the introduction, impact investors need to reframe their objectives to embrace the Genius of AND in order to move beyond the artificial dichotomy of financial return versus positive social and environmental impacts.

While certainly not an advocate of impact investing, David F. Swensen, the Chief Investment Officer of Yale University and the author of *Pioneering Portfolio Management*, offers these investment suggestions which we think are also applicable to impact investors. Swensen writes that "…a rich understanding of human psychology, a reasonable appreciation of financial theory, a deep awareness of history, and a broad exposure to current events all contribute to the development of well informed portfolio strategies."[9] Throughout this chapter, it is our intent to illustrate how the impact investor, embracing the Genius of AND, can successfully develop and execute a rigorous approach to applying existing portfolio theory and investment discipline. First, we return to the cornerstone of traditional investment principles: asset allocation.

Asset Allocation Basics

Asset allocation is an approach in which investors spread investments over different asset categories, such as traditional stocks, bonds and cash along with what some call alternative investments (e.g., private equity, hedge funds, real estate and other commodity strategies). This allocation of assets hinges upon several factors, including investment objectives; attitudes toward risk and investing; desired return; age, income and tax bracket; time horizon; view on how various markets will perform in the short and long term; AND for the impact investor, desired environmental and/or social impact.

Asset allocation is based on the observation that different broad categories of investments have shown varying rates of return and levels of price volatility over time. By diversifying investments across several asset classes, investors may reduce risk and volatility while pursuing their return objectives. Generally, downturns in one investment class are expected to be tempered (or even offset) by favorable returns in another. Just as using different asset categories within a portfolio can reduce risk, an investor's choice of individual strategies or securities within an asset class can do the same. For instance, choosing stocks from different industries (e.g., automotive, high technology, retail or utilities) within the equity allocation can be less risky than investing all of the stock allocation in one industry or company.

F.B. Heron Foundation's Mission-Related Investment Approach

The F.B. Heron Foundation supports organizations that help low-income people to create and preserve wealth thereby helping them take control of their lives and make decisions for themselves and their families. The F.B. Heron Foundation pioneered the integration of mission-related investment across its asset allocation. They created a mission-related investment continuum to provide a framework within the foundation's overall asset allocation to use as a tool to evaluate mission-related investment opportunities. By viewing grants as part of a broader range of philanthropic tools available to foundations to create impact, F.B. Heron is able to seek out the best agents for achieving impact in a program area whether through a non-profit or for-profit opportunity. F.B. Heron has systematically built out its mission-related investment portfolio across a range of asset classes and program areas while increasing the total share of mission-related investments in its endowment. This expansion followed a clear investment discipline and conformed to the foundation's overall asset allocation policy, performance benchmarks and prudent underwriting practices.   *Source: F.B. Heron Foundation*

Asset Allocation and the Impact Investor

Impact investors often find themselves questioning their ability to successfully execute an impact investment portfolio approach across their entire asset allocation. When starting this process, one of the first questions to answer is whether you are a financial first or impact first investor, or perhaps both.

For the financial first investor, sound economic principles that simultaneously satisfy social and/or environmental criteria serve as the drivers of opportunities in the portfolio construction process. In doing so, the investor can recognize and separate factors which serve as inputs to the financial component of the asset allocation process from those that do not. Although important, the potential social and/or environmental impact should not influence the financial risk attributable to a given asset class or investment in the asset allocation modeling process.

For the impact first investor, positive attributes of a desired social or environmental impact may outweigh pure financial considerations in the ultimate decision to allocate to a given investment. An investor may choose to go beyond traditional philanthropy and grants to employ flexible, patient capital opportunities that reflect the investor's desire to leverage social and environmental programs. Nonetheless, choosing the impact first approach should not dismiss the inclusion, evaluation and consideration of the financial risk associated with the proposed investment within the asset allocation framework.[10]

In some cases, an investment may satisfy both impact first and financial first investors. Opportunities that have high financial, social and/or environmental return are scarcer, but should be easier to identify once a clear investment thesis and theory of change have been developed. The impact investor's next step is to decide if they will fully embrace the Genius of AND by integrating impact investments into the overall portfolio allocation as opposed to a *carve-out*, a dedicated pool of capital allocated outside the portfolio. A *carve-out* approach may be appropriate for someone new to impact investing, but a committed impact investor should implement an integrated strategy to fully realize the potential of this type of investing. In either case, all the fundamental allocation and investment principles apply. For the integrated approach, the investor's risk tolerance and existing target asset allocation should serve as the basis for the inclusion of impact investments. Regardless of the portfolio construction methodology, the integrated impact investor should evaluate and allocate investments within their defined investment policy.

If opting to use a *carve-out* approach, a risk profile, investment objective and target asset allocation should be developed for this portion of the portfolio. Although some investors envision replicating their overall asset allocation objectives within this segregated impact investment pool, there are often practical limitations in doing so. Asset size of the portfolio and potential cost of the investments are two such constraints. For example, the investment universe available to a $100 million portfolio is far different from that of a $2 million portfolio. Additionally, costs are typically higher for smaller or more retail-focused products. This higher cost may lead to other challenges which may ultimately limit the impact investor's ability to optimize for either the financial or social/environmental impact objectives they seek.

Whether choosing an integrated or *carve-out* approach, impact investors should develop asset allocations based on risk tolerance, liquidity profile, spending needs, other financial considerations AND impact objectives.

Relationship Between Risk and Return

In a well-functioning market, risk is relative to return. A major goal of designing and managing an investment portfolio is to maximize total return while keeping overall risk at an acceptable level. With the introduction of the additional dimension of impact, investors' perceptions and considerations of the risk and return relationship may be modified. The key is to recognize these potential shifts and ensure that the appropriate investment process is in place to treat each of these accordingly. For example, when adopting a financial first approach, capital market assumptions including forecasted return and risk should not be influenced by expected social and environmental impact. Inversely, the impact first investor should initiate the assessment process by validating a given investment's ability to meaningfully impact the desired themes and then validate the characteristics of the proposed economic model.

Furthermore, forecasting asset class returns, like any attempt to predict the future, is difficult. History provides the only measurable guide as to how asset classes behave under different economic environments. Unfortunately, focusing purely on the past to predict the future presents challenges when evaluating investments on both financial and impact dimensions. For example, five years ago, the long-term data on the risk-to-return ratio of real estate investments were attractive, and that has shifted. The investor should not only consider historical performance, but also current events, short- and mid-term forecasted economic activity, regulation, externalities and human psychology to formulate capital market assumptions. The relationship of risk versus return can be influenced not only by the characteristics of a given asset class exposure, but also by investment structure used to gain exposure to the asset class. For example, a senior debt investment with a large amount of subordinated debt below it has significantly reduced risk.

Measuring Financial Risk

Measuring or analyzing the risk associated with different investments enables the investor to determine the right mix of asset classes for a portfolio. Risk can be measured in a number of ways. One measure of risk is standard deviation, namely, how much an investment's price varies from its mean (average) return over time. The greater the standard deviation of an asset, the higher its highs and the lower its lows will be from its mean return. When considering two securities with the same expected return, a rational choice would be to buy the one with the lower standard deviation, because it carries less risk. This decision becomes more complex when the investor is faced with social and environmental considerations. These concepts of risk are not only applicable in the context of asset allocation modeling, but in the evaluation and comparison of similar investments. This notion is what is often referred to as "risk-adjusted rate of return." Investors, including impact investors, are wise to look at an investment's attractiveness by measuring how much risk is involved in producing the associated return. This is generally expressed as a number or rating. Liquidity is also a major factor in risk assessment.

Behavioral finance suggests some modifications to the traditional risk assessment framework described above by pointing out that psychological phenomena leave investors subject to systematic errors, which then are reflected in asset prices. The term sentiment is used to describe these errors. For instance, sentiment can cause some assets to be mispriced. Sentiment can impact the relationship between risk and realized returns. Notably, traditional measures of risk only capture the sensitivity of asset returns relative to the overall market, but not to sentiment.

Correlation: Diversifying Asset Classes to Reduce Risk

Combining different asset classes within a portfolio is called diversification. The goal of diversification is to build a portfolio with investment classes that offer different levels of risk and react differently to market events. By doing so, the investor strives to reduce overall risk and improve overall performance. Correlation measures the strength and direction of a linear relationship between the price movements of two asset classes over time. A well-diversified portfolio consists of asset classes that are not closely correlated to each other. Historically, an example has been stocks and bonds. On the other hand, if a portfolio consists of stock asset classes that include Large Cap, Mid Cap and Small Cap stocks, it is not well diversified because historically these stocks have tended to be closely correlated.

Microfinance and Correlation

Impact investors can pursue investment opportunities offered by impact themes which have less correlation to traditional asset classes. By providing access to capital and community development, the microfinance industry has grown to represent approximately $30 billion in investments. As demonstrated in their 2008 study of microfinance institutions (MFIs), Nicolas Krauss and Ingo Walter of New York University found MFIs showed significantly less correlation to global market risk, for all parameters analyzed. (See www.accion.org/Page.aspx?pid=958.) In another study conducted at the University of Liechtenstein, Oliver Oehri and colleagues tested portfolio optimization scenarios by substituting 5% of a selected asset class with a microfinance debt proxy for the period January 1996 through June 2008. They concluded that adding the microfinance debt fund reduced risk for defensive and balanced portfolios, regardless of the asset class being replaced. (See www.iamfi.com/documents/OehriMFPortfolioOptimization.pdf.)

Asset Class Framework

This monograph categorizes investments by describing their role in a diversified portfolio. We are not advocating for a definitive language or approach to asset allocation. The following asset classes (which would need to be appropriately weighted given an investor's risk profile, spending needs, liquidity preferences and time horizon) represent the role an asset class may play in the development of a given portfolio:

- Cash and Cash Alternatives represent a portfolio's principal source of liquidity for meeting spending needs. The use of certificate of deposits and/or pledging cash accounts for guarantees alters this portion of the portfolio's liquidity and requires appropriate adjustments.

- Notes, Other Debt Obligations, Bonds, Absolute Return and Low Equity-Correlated Strategies may preserve wealth and/or generate income. The idea of low equity-correlation does not necessarily suggest exclusion of an equity investment. It is simply referring to an investment's relationship and performance relative to the broader global equity capital market asset class.

- Public Equity, Equity Long/Short and Private Equity assets serve to grow wealth through exposure to risk and strategies benefiting from global economic activity.

- Real Estate, Commodities, Timber and other Real Assets can protect a given portfolio from the erosion of purchasing power brought on by inflation.

Mapping Impact Themes to Asset Classes

Once you have decided on and documented an impact thesis and themes, you must identify opportunities to express these themes

Illustrative Landscape of Impact Themes

Asset Classes

	Stable Assets		Growth Assets
	Cash / Cash Alternatives	Fixed Income	Public Equity
Climate Change	Green Bank Deposit	Tax-Exempt Green Bonds	Positive & Negative Screening
Energy		Screened Corporate Bonds	Exchange Traded Funds (ETFs)
Water		Corporate Infrastructure Bonds	Unit Investment Trust, Closed End Funds
Community Development	Community Bank CDs	Foreclosure Repair	Shareholder Proxy Voting
Social Enterprises		Social Enterprise Credit	Micro-Cap Listed Social Companies
Health & Wellness			
Sustainable Development	Trade Finance Guarantee / Deposit	Smart Growth Municipal Bonds	Thematic Screening
Education	Linked Deposit / Guarantee	Charter School Bonds	

Social, Environmental or Blended Impact Themes

Asset Classes

Growth Assets		Inflation Protection	
Hedge Funds	Private Equity	Real Estate	Commodities, Timber & Other Real Assets
CO_2 Trading	Clean Tech Venture Capital	Green REITs	
Renewable Energy	Energy Efficiency Venture Capital		Sustainable Feedstocks
Water Funds	Water Technology Venture Capital		Water Rights
Microfinance Institutions Debt / Equity	Community Development Venture Capital	Transportation — Smart Development Funds	Habitat Conservation
	Small & Medium Enterprise	Conservation / Ecotourism	
Structured Public Note	Consumer Product Venture Capital	Organic Farming	
Blended Debt Equity Hybrid Structures		Ranch Land, Agriculture	Sustainable Timber
	Education Private Equity	University Green Building	

in a given portfolio. The set of available impact investment options is determined by the breadth or narrowness of impact themes, geographic exposure requirements and other characteristics. It is important to consider that not all impact themes expressed through grants or other forms of philanthropy can be uniformly expressed in investible assets. We offer the preceding table as an illustrative example of how some common impact themes can be expressed across asset classes for a portfolio. When reviewing the matrix, you should note that each box represents not only a different financial risk reward characteristic, but also varying degrees of "impact" for the particular theme. This chart, of course, does not include *all* opportunities among exposures and themes, and as the field of impact investing expands, the opportunities across asset classes and impact themes will increase.

Applications Across Impact Themes

To illustrate, we will first examine the climate change theme as expressed in public equity screening versus private equity clean technology venture capital. An investor in a given fund or pool of large company stocks cannot account for the degree to which these companies mitigate their negative impact on climate or deliver innovative solutions to the problem. Although various methodologies exist to evaluate Environmental, Social and Governance (ESG) factors, most companies classified as Large-Cap tend to be diversified across multiple business lines. Each business group within the larger corporation may contribute to climate change by varying degrees. While the size, amount of readily available information and liquidity of a public-traded corporation may reduce financial risk, these same factors may make it more difficult to express a specific impact theme. In contrast, investment in clean tech venture capital may allow for greater identification and possible "purity" of the expression of the desired impact theme. A single private company or even a pool of companies comprising a venture capital fund will tend to focus their activities. This comes with the inherent additional financial risk associated with illiquid and/or early stage businesses.

It is important to note that the comparison of public equity versus private equity exposure would be irrelevant to the investor who does not have the risk appetite to be exposed to either asset class. For a conservative investor desiring to address climate change, the only appropriate financial first options may be green bonds or cash deposits in green banks. If a US foundation is utilizing PRIs, it may also consider environmental impact first options, such as a note/debt obligation to organizations providing capital for low carbon technologies and services in the developing world.

While the prior example contrasts impact among asset classes, this example focuses on the acceptable scope or degree of impact a given investment must have within the same asset class. When looking at water as a theme within public equities, many water funds hold General Electric (GE). Although GE is in the water business, it is estimated that water accounts for no more than 5% of its activities. However, given GE's size, it is still one of the major players in this sector. The investor will have to determine the minimum level of acceptable direct impact. Some impact investors may be satisfied with 5%; for others it may be 25%, 50% or 100% of activities in the desired impact area.

Microfinance illustrates how one theme or strategy may be represented across the continuum of financial and impact considerations. Although microfinance is categorized as an absolute return/low equity correlated strategy in the matrix, a microfinance strategy can range from grants to non-profits to private/public equity in fully commercial microfinance institutions. Microfinance options are so numerous that one can narrow the impact objectives to focus on particular geographies, the percentage of women served, or the type of lending offered.

Many of the issues raised by the previous examples can be best addressed through a well-documented investment policy statement and through research and due diligence.

As the impact investing industry has evolved, investment opportunities across asset classes and impact themes have proliferated. While many early impact investments such as affordable housing were concentrated in the debt asset class, opportunities now span most major asset classes, and there are enterprises and funds with long operating histories. To illustrate these investment opportunities, we have provided three impact investment profiles in the following chapter, a summary of additional investment profiles in the appendix and the details of these investment profiles on the web. For a description of additional impact investment opportunities in various asset classes, the interested reader may also consult *Investing for Impact: Case Studies Across Asset Classes*, a study recently released by Bridges Ventures and The Parthenon Group.

Developing the Investment Policy Statement

The investment policy statement serves as the operating manual for a given portfolio. It documents the portfolio's objectives and constraints and outlines the roles and responsibilities of

Excerpt from the RSF Social Finance's Impact Portfolio Guidelines:

Objectives
1. Long-term principal appreciation;
2. Minimal income generation;
3. Minimal liquidity for cash disbursements or grantmaking;
4. Moderate volatility;
5. Time horizon of 3 to 7 years; and
6. Social impact % goal of 100.

Constraints
Mission: RSF's goal is for the Impact Portfolio to consist solely of mission investments. RSF applies a mission perspective to all investments made in the Impact Portfolio. Mission content typically varies by type of investment, but generally follows these guidelines:

- **Public Equity:** Managers and funds integrate environmental, social and corporate governance criteria into the investment management process and/or are active in positive shareholder advocacy.
- **Private Equity:** Fund investments address tangible social or environmental problems through the products and services of the companies in which they invest and the way in which they are managed.
- **Absolute Returns:** Funds invest capital in ways that support social and environmental value.
- **Real Assets:** Fund investments are either intrinsically sustainable assets or are in more conventional assets (e.g., real estate), managed in a sustainable manner.
- **Fixed Income:** Managers and funds directly provide capital to projects and organizations providing social and environmental value.
- **Cash and Cash Equivalent:** Cash deposits are made in community development and environmental banks and a mission screen is applied to other cash securities.

Source: RSF Social Finance

fiduciaries and other interested parties. Some important characteristics of a successful policy include: achievable goals and objectives; an understandable document; reasonable guidelines; consensus of all concerned parties on the policy statement; and a policy which is dynamic in nature (i.e., it is designed to be fine-tuned and updated when appropriate).

By embracing the Genius of AND, the impact investor can integrate the appropriate elements of an impact investing strategy into the traditional components of an investment policy statement. The preceding example from RSF Social Finance's Impact Portfolio demonstrates the integration of impact criteria into two key parts of the investment policy statement, namely Investment Goals & Objectives and Investment Constraints.

Additional components of the investment policy statement that can benefit from the integration of your impact objectives are:

A Purpose Statement — this should include a social and/or environmental impact thesis along with guidelines on the use and purpose of impact first investments.

Roles and Responsibilities — define the 'who,' 'how' and standards for impact assessment during the investment evaluation and the ongoing performance reporting process. This is most important if external resources will be utilized in generating deal flow, due diligence, portfolio recommendations and reporting.

Asset Allocation Target/Ranges — this may include specific ranges for the availability of impact opportunities within a given asset class and necessary accommodation for desired impact first investment allocations, in particular those qualifying as PRIs for US foundations.

Performance Benchmarks — documentation for the use of equivalent risk-adjusted commercial benchmarks for the financial first allocation. The development of standards is important for impact first investments. Examples include: equivalent commercial benchmarks with a discount factor; the use of an absolute return hurdle; or commonly available measures such as the Consumer Price Index.

Here is another example of impact investors aligning their investment policy to achieve their desired financial results AND impact objectives. The KL Felicitas Foundation has established the following investment policy by asset class:

KL Felicitas Foundation Investment Policy Guidelines

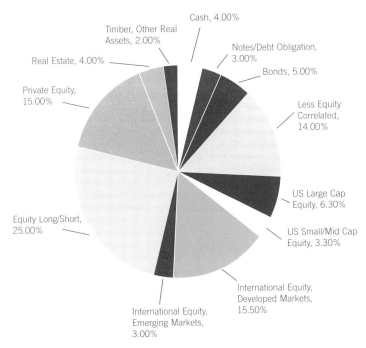

AND set the following objective of exposure to its impact categories, targeting a 100% impact portfolio by 2012. As of August 2009, the foundation has successfully deployed 21 impact investments committing over 55% of its portfolio.

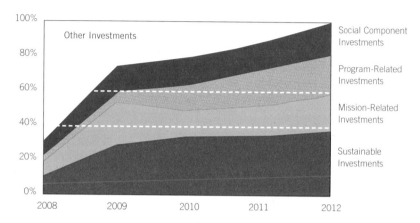

Portfolio Process Overview

Having developed an impact investing strategy as outlined in the preceding chapters and having articulated a target allocation and investment policy, your next steps are portfolio construction, implementation, ongoing monitoring and adjustment to the process as needed. Although the portfolio process will be covered in further detail in other chapters, we offer the following overview of key steps.

Financial First
optimal financial return
AND
acceptable social and/or
environmental return

Impact First
optimal social and/or
environmental impact
AND
acceptable financial return

PASS   EVALUATION PROCESS   PASS

Investment
Due Diligence

Social/Environmental
Assessment*

OR: consider

PASS

PASS

Social/Environmental
Assessment

Investment Due
Diligence

OR: consider as traditional investment

OR: consider for philanthropy/grant

PASS

PASS

Compliance with
Investment Policy
Statement

Compliance with
Investment Policy
Statement**

OR: consider for future allocation

OR: consider for future allocation

PASS   IMPLEMENTATION   PASS

Execution of required process and documentation

PASS   BENCHMARKING/REPORTING   PASS

Competitive risk adjusted rate
of return financial benchmark
for asset class and/or strategy
AND
acceptable social and/or
environmental impact
performance metrics

Acceptable social and/or
environmental impact
performance metrics
AND
predetermined financial
objective and/or assumed
financial return

* Program-Related Investment (PRI) consideration for US foundations
** Noted to Investment Policy Statement if PRI for US foundation

Investor Intent

The first step is to clarify your motivation and intent as an impact investor. Is it to maximize profits with demonstrated social and/or environmental benefits? Or is the objective to seek out the optimal impact solutions for the societal and/or environmental challenges? Or is it both?

Based on the answer to this question, you need to develop the pipeline of investment opportunities. Once the portfolio objectives of financial risk/return and impact are clearly defined and articulated in the investment policy statement, internal investment and/or program staff, external advisors and consultants, fund managers and/or other resources will be able to identify the appropriate opportunities.

Financial First Investors

For the financial first investor, once deal flow has been generated, an appropriate quantitative and qualitative investment due diligence process should be completed. It is important that this process mirrors standards set for similar asset classes and strategies of non-impact investments. For example, the process associated with evaluating an impact certificate of deposit, which is FDIC-insured and issued by a community bank, may involve a simple comparison of rates available in the market. Due diligence may be simply accessing publicly available information on the issuing bank and calling a bank representative. On the other hand, if the investment under consideration is a highly illiquid strategy, such as private real estate, offered by a first-time fund manager, the process will be far more complex. This would most likely include several meetings with the management team, thorough financial analysis of any historical, current or projected transactions, background checks on the principals, and extensive legal review of the offering documents and operational assessment of the management company.

If the investment fails to successfully complete the financial due diligence process, but appears to exhibit meaningful social or environmental impact, it can be directed for consideration within the impact first process.

Assuming the proposed financial first investment has successfully completed the appropriate investment due diligence, an evaluation of the social and/or environmental impact should be completed. The extent of social and/or environmental impact should be articulated in the investment policy statement. You may choose to accept the impact metrics currently offered by the fund/investment, develop agreed-upon standards for reporting, or use third party tools or service providers for the impact evaluation process. If the investment fails to address and/or provide the desired impact, the investment is removed from consideration, but may be considered in the context of traditional (non-impact related) investing.

For the impact investment which has successfully completed both financial and impact analysis, the next step is to consult the investment policy and determine appropriate size and timing within the context of the current portfolio holdings/asset allocation. If compliant with policy, the investment would simply proceed with an investor's implementation protocols. If not compliant, whether due to current exposure limits, geography or other constraints, the investment would not be implemented and should be considered for future allocation. The investment could be implemented once the limiting factors have been removed and any updates to the analysis are completed.

Impact First Investors:

If you are an impact first investor, the process should begin with the evaluation of the proposed social and/or environmental impact. As discussed in Chapter 8 in more detail, many methods exist to address this. If the proposed impact investment fails this process, it should be removed from consideration.

Investments satisfying the desired impact criteria move into the investment due diligence process. Once again, an appropriate level of quantitative and qualitative analysis should be conducted relative to the complexity, liquidity and risk associated with the proposed investment. Sometimes investors are quick to overlook the financial merits of an opportunity presenting compelling social and/or environmental impact. In doing so they may overlook the risk associated with a flawed economic model. This could ultimately result in the failure or the lack of scalability of the investment, negating the ability to achieve the sought-after impact.

At the same time, extenuating circumstances may cause a proposed impact first investment to fail the investment due diligence process but still meet the test of creating meaningful impact. In such cases, pure philanthropic capital may be considered to fund the initiative until it is more mature and able to accommodate impact investment capital.

Impact first investments satisfying the impact assessment and investment due diligence must then be considered within the framework of the investment policy. For US foundations qualifying the proposed allocation as a Program Related Investment (PRI) and counting it as a portion of the required spending, simply noting the allocation to the investment policy should suffice. This is a result of the PRI being a substitution of the foundation's greatest risk capital — grants — something that would currently be captured as spending within the investment policy and portfolio-modeling framework.

For investors not able to qualify the proposed investment as a PRI, compliance with the guidelines established by the investment policy should be adhered to. As before, if current constraints or portfolio holdings prevent compliance with policy, the investment will be considered for future allocation. The investment could be implemented once the limiting factors have been removed and any updates to the analysis are completed.

Although not illustrated in the process diagram, you should note that impact funds, investment structures and hybrid enterprises might offer tranches that fit within financial first, impact first and philanthropic options. What may start as the exploration of an opportunity in one area may quickly find its way to another or may even be satisfied with capital from multiple funding sources. In either case the appropriate process should be applied relative to the role and purpose of the available capital.

By harnessing the Genius of AND, we believe you can not only apply financial portfolio theory, but can also benefit from applying the discipline of asset allocation, investment policy statements and a rigorous, well-defined portfolio process.

---

9 Swensen, David, *Pioneering Portfolio Management: An Unconventional Approach to Institutional Investment*, New York: Free Press, 2000.

10 Given the specific treatment under US tax law of Program-Related Investments made by US foundations, PRIs may be considered a portion of the required charitable distribution rather than the asset allocation. By substituting the greatest risk capital of the foundation — that of a grant — and modifying the actual spending policy, PRIs need only be noted within the target asset allocation and portfolio investment policy.

Chapter 6:

Generating Deal Flow

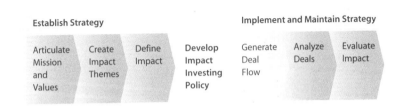

Establish Strategy

Implement and Maintain Strategy

| Articulate Mission and Values | Create Impact Themes | Define Impact | Develop Impact Investing Policy | Generate Deal Flow | Analyze Deals | Evaluate Impact |

Building the Transaction Pipeline

Once you have defined your impact themes, developed your impact investment policy and an appropriate asset allocation, the challenge shifts to finding and executing impact investment transactions. Your success will depend on your search efforts, your advisors, the ability to tap resources and the ability to build a network of relationships. Actively pursuing investment opportunities will result in a very different universe of investment opportunities than waiting for proposals. Your co-investors may include a broad range of investors such as insurance companies, banks, pension funds, endowments and individuals. The public sector may also participate directly as a co-investor or indirectly through credit enhancement or refinancing of specific transactions. Information-sharing networks can bring important benefits by disbursing information and increasing familiarity with impact investing among potential investors. Impact investors are also forming networks such as the Global Impact Investing Network

(GIIN), More for Mission and impact investment collaboratives in which impact investors share expertise and co-investment opportunities. (See www.rockpa.org/impactinvesting for a listing of resources.) While reviewing impact investment opportunities, also keep in mind that supply and demand need to co-evolve in this market. Investors need to understand how they can assist in the mentoring, incubation and acceleration of impact investment opportunities to avoid a market in which the available capital exceeds the available supply of high-quality deals.

Direct Versus Funds Strategy

The decision to make direct investments and/or to utilize funds and other types of intermediaries is a critical step in the execution of your impact investing strategy. The decision to utilize a direct and/or fund-driven approach may be a function of your impact themes and desired level of engagement in the investment process. For example, in the impact themes of affordable housing and microfinance, there is a wide range of funds through which an investor could invest. In other sectors investors may have to work to create and seed such funds or look to investment opportunities with secondary or tertiary effects related to a primary impact theme (e.g., the impact on health through a microfinance investment). The due diligence process will differ between direct investment and funds as well.

Fund Investment Selection Criteria

The Calvert Community Investment Note
Through its Community Investment Note program (Notes),

Calvert Foundation invests in non-profits with proven track records that demonstrate strong management, effective operations, good financial performance and sound capitalization. Borrowers are subject to a rigorous due diligence process. Calvert Foundation has designed Notes to be suitable for all classes of investors, from large institutions and high net-worth individuals looking to leverage a portion of their investment portfolio towards community development initiatives, to retail social investors seeking to align their investment decisions more seamlessly with their values. Notes are a taxable, low-volatility fixed-income product. Notes provide accessible capital to community development organizations around the world while offering investors a compelling blend of social and financial return; therefore they are a suitable addition to both investment portfolios and philanthropic portfolios.

RSF Donor-Advised Funds Investment Portfolios
RSF's goal is to identify and invest in the most direct opportunities available to support innovative funds, institutions and projects, reducing unnecessary levels of intermediation, while also meeting diversification, risk and return criteria. Social impact is measured by a combination of quantitative and qualitative factors with a focus on the outputs of the investments such as the number of affordable housing units financed, low-income mortgages made and environmental impacts achieved.

Current Universe of Impact Investment Funds

To aid current and prospective impact investors and their advisors with developing a framework for evaluating investments, we have provided an "Impact Investment Profile" template on page 84 which can be customized to evaluate impact investing opportunities. Using this form, we have included three Impact Investment Profiles in this chapter. Additional Impact Investment Profiles, which were produced over the course of our research, have been made available at www.rockpa.org/impactinvesting.

The profiles featured in this chapter and the case studies in the following chapter are representative examples of the more than 100 funds and enterprises our team researched for this publication. We have evaluated and documented each example using the same criteria for social and environmental impact areas, asset classes and geographic exposures. Given the pioneering nature of the impact investing industry, some of these funds may lack the investment track record and benchmarked performance data of more traditional investment approaches. Offsetting these risks are the increasingly impressive track records of the fund managers themselves and the accumulating evidence of what works and what does not work in impact investing. Please note that we are by no means providing an exhaustive database of deal flow, nor are we offering investment advice, but rather we are seeking to show meaningful deal flow across multiple asset classes.

Other efforts like the Global Impact Investing Network (GIIN) database project have embarked on creating a comprehensive database of impact investment offerings. The GIIN open access database seeks to present over 1,000 impact investment opportunities — funds and products — in a format that can be sorted, viewed and used by investors and intermediaries (see www.globalimpactinvestingnetwork.org).

Methodology Used

Impact investment opportunities have social/environmental and financial dimensions. Our template is careful to highlight both aspects of the funds and enterprises. The profile has four main parts: a table with a snapshot of the proposed impact and investment; an overview of the impact to identify the problem/need; a description of the market; and the investment's proposed response. Furthermore, the language utilized in completing the table of the profiles has been aligned with the taxonomy developed by GIIN for their upcoming database.

The final section presents basic information on the fund or investment, including the appropriate contact person. This information was obtained from the supporting documentation of profiled funds. In most instances, funds were easily categorized in a particular asset class. In some cases, however, funds made both debt and equity investments and thus had characteristics of more than one asset class. In such cases, the funds are simply noted as Multi-Asset. Although behavioral dimensions of the funds and enterprises are not addressed on the profiles, the information presented on the fund or enterprise allows a prospective investor to evaluate different behavioral elements of the investment opportunities, illustrating why certain classes of funds and enterprises have not historically received funding or attention from investors.

The content in these profiles was derived from information provided by the profiled investment opportunities and our team.

Impact Investment Profile

Template

Impact	Investment
Approach: *Financial First, Impact First or Hybrid*	**Asset Class:** *Cash, Cash Alternatives, Guarantees, Notes/Debt Obligations, Bonds, Absolute Return/Low Equity Correlated Strategies, Public Equity, Equity Long/Short, Private Equity, Real Estate, Commodities, Timber, Other Real Assets, Multi-Asset*
Theme: *Social, Environmental, Blended or Other*	**Structure:** *Fund, Fund of Funds, Separate Account, Security*
Sector: Social *— Social Enterprises, Community Development, Corporate Social Responsibility* **Environmental** *— Green Technology/ Cleantech, Environmental Markets and Sustainable Real Assets, Sustainable Consumer Products*	**Status:** *Exploratory, Actively Raising, Closed*
Sub-sector: Community Development *— Affordable Housing, Small Business, Community Facilities, Rural Development/Agriculture, Base of the Pyramid, Microfinance, Small & Medium Enterprises* **Corporate Social Responsibility** *— ESG Analysis, Screening, Shareholder Advocacy* **Environmental Markets and Sustainable Real Assets** *— Carbon & Environmental Markets, Commodities, Conservation Finance, Water Quality & Rights Trading, Green Real Estate, Sustainable Forestry, Sustainable Agriculture* **Green Technology/Cleantech** *— Energy, Fuels & Generation, Energy Efficiency, Transportation, Water Technology, Waste Management/Recycling, Materials Science* **Social Enterprise** *— Health, Education, The Arts, Human Rights, Social Services, Digital Access/New Media, Financial Services* **Sustainable Consumer Products** *— Green Consumer Products, Alternative Healthcare, Technology & Media, Food Products/Organics*	**Geography:** *US, North America, Latin/South America, Europe, Asia, Africa, Oceana, Global (Developed or Developing)*

1. Impact Overview

    a. Problem/Need:

    b. Description of the Market:

    c. Investment's Response to Market:

2. Fund/Investment Information

    a. Manager Name:

    b. Location:

    c. Fund Name:

    d. Firm Assets Under Management (AUM): *(asset size of parent organization)*

    e. Strategy AUM: *(asset size of particular strategy or venture)*

    f. Strategy Description:

    g. Key Individuals and Backgrounds:

    h. Portfolio Diversification:

    i. Fees:

    j. Liquidity:

    k. Minimum Investment:

    l. Contact:

Impact Investment Profile
E+Co People & Planet Note Series

Impact	Investment
Approach: Impact First	Asset Class: Notes/Other Debt Obligations
Theme: Blended	Structure: Fund
Sector: Social Enterprises, Community Development, Green Technology/ Cleantech	Status: Actively Raising
Sub-sector: Small and Medium Enterprises, Energy	Geography: Africa, Asia and Latin America

1. Impact Overview

a. <u>Problem/Need</u>: Developing markets lack enterprises that produce clean, sustainable energy, and energy demand often outpaces energy supply. Additionally, small- and medium-sized enterprises in these areas often lack access to funding to develop or scale their operations.

b. <u>Description of the Market</u>: E+Co's portfolio enterprises provide energy to 6.2 million people in Asia, Africa, and Latin America. E+Co seeks to scale up this effort to deliver energy to an additional 17 million people. These investments are in areas that use fossil fuels as a source of energy, which results in significant air pollution.

c. <u>Investment's Response to Market</u>: Investment allows for growth and development of clean energy enterprises, reducing the dependence of rural inhabitants in developing countries on fossil fuels for energy, increasing their energy supply and self-sufficiency, as well as contributing to a cleaner environment and bringing about sustainable community economic development.

2. Fund/Investment Information

a. <u>Manager Name</u>: E+Co (www.eandco.net)

b. <u>Location</u>: Bloomfield, NJ

c. <u>Fund Name</u>: People + Planet Notes Series

d. <u>Firm AUM</u>: $28.8 million as of December 31, 2008

e. Strategy AUM: $50 million target
f. Strategy Description: E+Co is issuing notes to raise capital for investments in modern energy enterprises in developing countries. E+Co seeks to establish sustainable energy businesses that serve the energy poor and create non-financial social as well as environmental benefits. The notes will be offered with an 8-year maturity, paying 3% annually.
g. Key Individuals and Backgrounds: Christine Eibs Singer, Chief Executive Officer, 25 years' experience in design, implementation of public-private partnerships, including UN Foundation REED (Rural Energy Enterprise Development) programs with UNEP, and Port Authority of NY and NJ
h. Portfolio Diversification: 268 energy enterprises currently in portfolio, located in Africa (33%), Asia (40%) and Latin America (27%). Seeks an additional 300 investments by 2012.
i. Fees: None
j. Liquidity: Eight year maturity, depending on the note structure
k. Minimum Investment: $100,000 subject to manager discretion
l. Contact: Meredith Elliott, meredith.elliott@eandco.net

Impact Investment Profile
Neuberger Berman Socially Responsive Equity

Impact	Investment
Approach: Financial First	Asset Class: Public Equity
Theme: Social	Structure: Fund, Separate Account
Sector: Corporate Social Responsibility	Status: Actively Raising
Sub-sector: ESG Analysis, Screening	Geography: US

1. Impact Overview

a. Problem/Need: Sustainability challenges relating to business include the depletion of natural resources, the failure of companies to adequately monitor their corporate citizenship practices, companies' participation in industries that offer or introduce negative externalities to society and the continued efforts needed to enhance workplace diversity.

b. Description of the Market: Neuberger Berman selects mid- and large-cap stocks typically traded on US exchanges.

c. Investment's Response to Market: The Fund highlights companies that best approach issues of good governance and corporate citizenship, increasing the importance of these criteria for investors, and in turn bringing about positive social change through large companies. Companies should demonstrate leadership in the areas of environmental impact, workplace practices, community relations, innovative products & design, and management practices to drive longer-term sustainability and robustness of the business strategy.

2. Fund/Investment Information

a. Manager Name: Neuberger Berman (www.nb.com)

b. Location: New York, NY

c. Fund Name: Neuberger Berman Socially Responsive Equity

d. Firm AUM: $180 billion, as of 3/31/2010

e. Strategy AUM: $3.8 billion total, $1.2 billion in the Fund as of 3/31/2010

f. Strategy Description: An open-ended mutual fund that invests in shares of listed equity securities that meet financial as well as social criteria. The fund has a value bias, and seeks out companies with secularly advantaged growth prospects that show leadership in major areas of social impact such as the environment, workplace diversity and progressive employment practices. The fund invests mainly in common stocks of mid- to large-capitalization companies. It seeks to reduce risk by investing across many different industries. The fund looks for solid balance sheets, strong management teams with a track record of success, good cash flow, the prospect for above average earnings growth and other valuation-related factors. The fund does not invest in companies that derive revenue from gambling, alcohol, tobacco, firearms or nuclear power.

g. Key Individuals and Backgrounds: Arthur Moretti, 23 years in industry, portfolio manager since 2001; Ingrid Saukaitis Dyott, 15 years in industry, portfolio manager since 2003. Mamundi Subhas, Associate Portfolio Manager. Sajjad Ladiwala, Associate Portfolio Manager.

h. Portfolio Diversification: 31 listed equities as of 3/31/2010 selected from among approximately 900 mid- and large-cap stocks on listed exchanges in the US

i. Fees: .78% expense ratio (institutional), 1.17% expense ratio (Class A)

j. Liquidity: Daily

k. Minimum Investment: NBSLX $1 million (institutional), NRAAX $1,000 (Class A)

l. Contact: William Timmons, william.timmons@nb.com

The information presented herein has been prepared for informational purposes only and is not an offer to buy or sell, or a solicitation of an offer to buy or sell, any security or fund interest. The offering circular of each security or the respective fund's confidential offering memorandum contains important information concerning risks and other material aspects of the investment and must be read carefully before a decision to invest is made.

Although the information presented herein has been obtained from and is based upon sources we believe to be reliable, no representation or warranty, express or implied, is made as to the accuracy or completeness of that information. No assurance can be given that the investment objectives described herein will be achieved.

Impact Investment Profile
Zouk Cleantech Europe II

Impact	Investment
Approach: Financial First	Asset Class: Private Equity
Theme: Environmental	Structure: Fund
Sector: Green Technology/Cleantech	Status: Actively Raising
Sub-sector: Multiple	Geography: Europe

1. Impact Overview

a. Problem/Need: The effects of climate change continue to impact the environment, global population growth continues to fuel increased energy demand, natural resource depletion threatens conventional energy supply, and impending governmental regulations and incentives encourage investment in sustainable energy production.

b. Description of the Market: As the early adopter, Europe is an entrenched, fast-developing market with long-term regulations. Europe has also outpaced other regions (61 billion euros, over 40% of global total in 2008). Limited competition for deals, tight pricing discipline and large localized markets offer a strong private equity environment.

c. Investments Response to Market: Fund to provide growth equity and active support to technology companies in alternative & renewable energy, resource efficiency and environmental services technology filling an established and increasing demand in Europe.

2. Fund/Investment Information

a. Manager Name: Zouk Ventures (www.zouk.com)

b. Location: London, UK

c. Fund Name: Cleantech Europe II, LP

d. Firm AUM: 190 million euros across three funds (excl. Cleantech Europe II)

e. Strategy AUM: Cleantech Europe II is targeting 200 million euros in LP commitments

f. Strategy Description: Cleantech Europe II is a private equity fund that will invest primarily in European, expansion stage clean-tech companies with commercially proven technology. Zouk will actively manage its portfolio companies, leveraging its proven track record of providing strategic, business development and financial structuring support.

g. Key Individuals and Backgrounds: Zouk has been building businesses since 1999, with the partners working together for an average of six years. Samer Salty, CEO and co-founder, Boards: Solarcentury and Orb Energy, formerly JPMorgan M&A and PE; Felix von Schubert, partner and co-founder, Boards: Sulfurcell Solartechnik, Nanotron Technologies, The CarbonNeutral Company and Zooplus, formerly JPMorgan, M&A and PE; Alois Flatz, partner, Board: SiC Processing, former head of research at SAM, founder of Dow Jones Sustainability Index; Anthony Fox, Board: Trilliant, ex CEO Kingfisher E-Commerce Plc and a handful of business-building roles across Asia and the Middle East

h. Portfolio Diversification: Target of 10-15 investments

i. Fees: 2.5% (of total commitment) management fee from first closing for five years, then declining 0.25% per year, plus 20% carried interest over an 8% hurdle rate

j. Liquidity: Fund has eight-year life, plus two one-year extensions

k. Minimum Investment: 5 million euros, subject to manager discretion

l. Contact: Philip Tomlin, philiptomlin@zouk.com

UNEP FI's Environmental and Social Responsibility Observatory

The United Nations Environment Programme Finance Initiative (UNEP FI) is a strategic public-private partnership between UNEP and the global financial sector. UNEP FI works with over 180 banks, insurers and investment firms, and a range of partner organizations to understand the impacts of environmental, social and governance issues on financial performance and sustainable development. Through a comprehensive work program encompassing research, training and region-specific activities, UNEP FI carries out its mission to identify, promote and realize the adoption of best environmental and sustainability practices at all levels of financial institution operations.

In support of its efforts, UNEP FI has embarked on the development of a case study database — the Environmental and Social Responsibility Observatory (ESRO). ESRO will be an innovative online database for financial analysts, investors and lenders looking for case studies at the intersection of commercial finance, investment and sustainability. Ranging across geographies, industries and sustainability issues, these case studies can demonstrate the financial benefits of appropriate environmental and social risk management in financial decision-making. The database should prove to be a helpful tool for impact investors as they evaluate a landscape of historical transactions, identify experienced players and source new opportunities. For additional information, visit www.unepfi.org.

Generating deal flow is an ongoing and evolving process. Investment managers, product designers, intermediaries and often impact investors themselves are continually developing offerings to harness the scale and power of capital markets to deliver solutions to the social and environmental challenges faced by society. These efforts are not only underway in the boardrooms of the traditional financial or philanthropic centers, but are occurring at the grassroots level throughout the developing world, where many of the desired "impact" objectives are felt in real time. This results in deal sourcing being a global effort as impact investors seek opportunities to satisfy their desired levels of financial return AND social/ environmental impact.

Impact Investing Conferences

Impact investors seeking investment opportunities, thoughtful leadership, peer learning and collaboration benefit from a growing number of dedicated conferences and events. Examples which have demonstrated repeatedly the ability to convene audiences and offer insights and opportunities across the spectrum of impact investing include:

- PRI Makers Network National Conference (www.primakers.net/conference)
- Take Action! Impact Investing Conference Series (www.takeactionforimpact.com)
- TBLI Conference (www.tbliconference.com)
- SOCAP Annual Conference (www.socialcapitalmarkets.net)

Chapter 7:

Analyzing Deals

| Articulate Mission and Values | Create Impact Themes | Define Impact | Develop Impact Investing Policy | Generate Deal Flow | Analyze Deals | Evaluate Impact |

Due Diligence of Impact Investments

Due diligence is your organization's research and investigation of impact investment opportunities. A first step in this process is to answer threshold questions such as:

- What is the impact investment thesis for this opportunity and how does it further specific impact goals?
- Is this a financial first or impact first investment?
- Who are the principals involved in the investment?
- Does the transaction leverage other sources of capital?
- What are the impact and financial risks and how are they distributed?
- Will this investment enable a project to happen that otherwise would not?
- Are there behavioral finance aspects you should consider?
- Does the investment raise reputation or policy issues?
- Where would this transaction fit in your overall asset allocation?

After an initial review, you and/or your financial advisor will complete a full review of the financial statements or offering documents and other relevant organizational materials as well as project-specific documentation such as projections and business plans. For some impact investment opportunities, it is possible to purchase "off-the-shelf" financial analysis from third party providers. Keep in mind that structured investments such as project financings, loan funds or investment in private equity funds will require a more customized financial analysis. A clear assessment of the quality of the management team is a key element of the due diligence. When investing in an intermediary, it is necessary to assess the fund manager's ability to find portfolio companies and projects that fit your impact and investment goals. You may look to a fund manager's previous track record with placing and exiting investments as one indicator of future success.

In general, financial advisors and other investment intermediaries will be more comfortable assessing the financial risk of the investment. The due diligence process for impact investments also needs to consider potential "impact risks" and their mitigation. Careful consideration of the mission-alignment of the management is crucial. So too is attention to the governance structure of the fund or company and how it will inform the inevitable trade-offs that successful impact investments encounter between opportunities for financial gain and impact. For direct investments, this additional due diligence can add substantial transaction costs. The deeper engagement by investment principals which this approach necessitates should be seen as more than simply an increase in research costs. Engagement with the management team often provides additional motivation and reward for the impact investor as well as for the investment. Options are also available to reduce transaction costs, most notably by investing through an established intermediary that aggregates investors' capital, such as the case of the Triodos Sustainable Trade Fund described below.

Investment Processes

Calvert Foundation:
Because the Calvert Community Investment Note is a debt instrument, Calvert Foundation's due diligence is based on an intensive credit underwriting that examines the applicant's credit quality, considering organizational history and mission, management and board, operating capacity, asset quality, and capitalization, among other criteria. This due diligence is performed by a team of outside analysts and is supported by an experienced in-house team. The foundation performs annual due diligence on all of its borrowers in order to remain fully apprised of their financial positions and operating conditions. Quarterly financial statements are required of all borrowers. For borrowers on the Watch List, additional monitoring is performed.

Based on the due diligence process, Calvert Foundation allocates a specific risk-rating category to each investment to determine the loan loss provision associated with that investment. Specific loan loss reserve requirements have been established for each internal risk tranche in the portfolio. Calvert Foundation's Board Investment Committee carefully monitors repayment history and actual experience to ensure the overall portfolio is performing and reserved appropriately. Individual positions are constantly reviewed for creditworthiness against the above guidelines and for the social impact the loans are creating.

KL Felicitas Foundation:

At KL Felicitas, the investment process follows a clear flow chart identifying the critical path action items and responsibility among the trustees and their advisors. The process varies depending on the type of impact investing (Sustainability Investments, Mission-Related Investments, Program-Related Investments and Social Component Investments). You can find detailed process descriptions at www.klfelicitasfoundation.org. KL Felicitas' MRI Evaluator tool is designed to work in conjunction with a formal investment due diligence process. It allows a foundation to assess, document and define roles for evaluating any given investment opportunity in the areas of:

• Investment structure, portfolio implications and financial performance reporting;
• Alignment with Mission or Purpose; and
• Establishing Mission 'Impact' criteria.

Impact investors may be as detailed as they like in documenting responses to the Evaluator tool questions. A scoring system is included for each question, allowing the impact investor to establish a more objective framework for evaluating impact investments. It is important to document a pass or fail scale for scoring results. KL Felicitas uses a very simple scoring system of -1, 0, and +1 to determine if a given investment is compliant, neutral, or not compliant with the various guidelines and objectives as expressed in the questions of the Evaluator tool.

RSF Social Finance's Core Lending Investment Process:

Loan inquiries are initially vetted by RSF's relationship managers and, once qualified, the due diligence is prepared. This work includes traditional loan underwriting, but also evaluates the social entrepreneur's intention for beginning the business, potential exit strategies, and plans for improving production and supply chains from a social impact perspective. The Credit Committee reviews first the intention(s) of the entrepreneur and the social impact to ensure alignment with RSF's values and strategic plan, and then the underwriting is reviewed. If approved, RSF has a board-approved Loan Authorities Matrix for obtaining the required signatures for closing. Day-to-day management of loan clients is the responsibility of the individual relationship managers.

Pico Bonito Investment Process

KL Felicitas' investment in Pico Bonito followed these steps:

- The Kleissners visited one of EcoLogic's projects in Guatemala and were impressed by the organization's approach and results.
- When one of EcoLogic's founders alerted the Kleissners of an investment opportunity in a 'spin-off' called Pico Bonito, the Kleissners were interested in learning more.
- Initial high level due diligence with the founders of Pico Bonito indicated that this could be a Mission-Related Investment (financial first investment), as the overall goals of Pico Bonito were very much in alignment with the mission of the foundation. The Kleissners asked their investment advisor to complete appropriate financial due diligence.
- The financial due diligence resulted in a recommendation to re-evaluate this possible investment as a Program-Related Investment or impact first investment.
- Based on the rest of the due diligence process, the board approved a Program-Related Investment into Pico Bonito as well as a grant to EcoLogic.

Due Diligence Case Studies

At the core of the due diligence process is the analysis of the underlying impact investment business models and risks. We have included the Triodos Sustainable Trade Fund (TSTF) and the Indian healthcare social enterprise Dial 1298 for Ambulance in order to provide a deeper understanding of impact first business models and the aspects of due diligence an impact investor might undertake. In each case we have outlined the organization's mission, the problem they are addressing, their business model and the challenges and opportunities they face. TSTF is a guarantee fund providing financing to fair trade producers around the world. Dial 1298 for Ambulance is an operating social enterprise. If your impact investment is made through a fund, the underlying social enterprises in the fund's portfolio will also have to be analyzed because your desired social and environmental impacts are created at the enterprise level. We have selected Dial 1298 for Ambulance to demonstrate the components of a social enterprise investment opportunity.

Background Brief

Triodos Sustainable Trade Fund (TSTF) provides trade financing for certified fair trade and organic (CFT/O) producers. The fund provides developing world CFT/O farmers and farmer cooperatives willing to adopt more sustainable methods with a cash flow bridge loan from the start of the harvest season to the receipt of revenue from exported goods. These loans are collateralized by the receivables under the export contracts. Investors can participate by either providing a guarantee or a subordinated loan. TSTF is a special purpose fund of Triodos Bank, a leading sustainable bank in Europe. TSTF grew out of Triodos Bank's prior efforts in microfinance and trade finance for producers in developing countries.

Mission

Triodos Bank's mission is to help create a society that promotes people's quality of life and that has human dignity at its core; to enable individuals, institutions and businesses to use money more consciously in ways that benefit people and the environment and promote sustainable development; and to offer its customers sustainable financial products and high quality service.

Problem and/or Need

The most significant challenge commonly faced by farming industry participants is the bridging of cash flow from the start of the harvest season to receipt of revenue from exported goods. Farmers and cooperatives often lack the capacity to adequately train and manage farmers and employees. They often also have limited access to international and/or domestic capital markets, and lack the knowledge required to address increasing demands for their goods. From 2005 to 2006, there was a 41% increase in consumer expenditures on fair-trade certified products, according to the Fairtrade Labelling Organizations (FLO) — with cocoa, coffee and tea demand leading growth figures. The nations served by TSTF are underdeveloped as defined by the OECD. Often, they have significant obstacles to foreign investment, including underdeveloped or inadequate banking and securities industry regulations, unstable or high levels of inflation and significant foreign currency risk.

TSTF's opportunity exists because developing countries are and have been underserved by traditional financial capital markets. In industrialized countries, it is typical for merchants to obtain trade financing to provide cash flow before and in anticipation of sales of their goods. In developing countries, there is often no such financing available, nor is there any price guarantee once the selling/exporting season begins.

Business Model

The Investors

The Triodos Sustainable Trade Fund has raised 8 million euros of guarantees and is actively seeking to raise additional subordinated loans. Investors in the fund place euro-based deposits (minimum of 250,000 euros) with Triodos Bank (TB), which currently pays between 2% and 3%. The deposits are then pledged and provided as guarantees for the bank thereby leveraging the funds by a factor of three. The bank then lends these enhanced proceeds to the Triodos Sustainable Trade Fund. Due to the low profitability of such a trade finance portfolio and the inability of TSTF to offer a reasonable risk-adjusted return to its investors, the Fund is structured as a not-for-profit foundation.

The Fund makes a gross margin of around 2.5% and a net margin of around 1% on the loans disbursed to borrowers. The fund is also subject to a 2.5% fund management fee on loans disbursed to Triodos Investment Management BV. The costs are passed on to the Fund's clients as an administration fee.

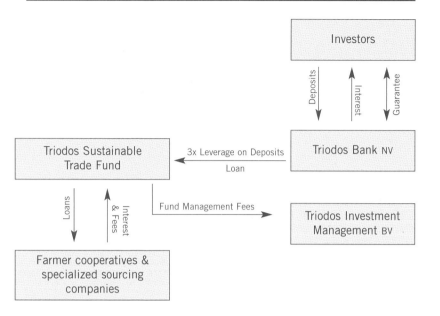

In the event of default by underlying borrowers to the TSTF, the losses are shared by and charged to the pledged deposits (guarantors) held by Triodos Bank. Over the past five years, according to Triodos, only two losses have been reported, amounting to less than 1% of the average amount of loans disbursed. It is important to note that although Triodos Bank provides three times leverage to the TSTF, investors' capital at risk is equal only to the amount of their deposit.

The performance (likelihood of default) of guarantees is uncorrelated to other securities, as its interest payments are dependent on successful harvests in emerging markets. The risks therein are isolated from capital markets in industrialized countries, and as such the security provides portfolio diversification.

The Borrower
The start of the loan period coincides with the start of the harvesting season and may continue until the last shipment of the exported products. Usually the loan duration is between 6 and 12 months.

Amounts financed depend on the cash-flow needs of the exporting company and are based on a percentage of the value of the export contracts. For fresh crops this percentage is generally no more than 40%. For less vulnerable produce, such as coffee and cocoa, this percentage can be as high as 60%.

Triodos Sustainable Trade Fund charges a floating interest rate, consisting of the 1-month Euribor or Libor rate, plus a client specific interest spread. The loan is generally denominated in the currency of the export contract, typically either in euros or US dollars. After all conditions stipulated in the loan agreement are fulfilled, the loan amount is either disbursed in full or in tranches. Collateral beyond the receivables related to the export contracts is usually not required.

When payment under the export contract becomes due, the buyer transfers his payments into a Triodos bank account. Triodos withholds a certain percentage of these payments as repayment of the loan and transfers the remaining amount into the account of the exporting company.

Social & Environmental Impact

According to Triodos Investment Management's (TIM) metrics, guarantees supporting the TSTF have a multiplier effect in terms of their impact on exporting contract value financed, sales revenue generated by farmers and premium income earned by farmers. TIM projects that every euro pledged as a guarantee will result in three euros disbursed as loans, five euros worth of sales generated by farmers, and 0.4 euro of premium income earned annually by farmers. The result is that farmers' premium income will amount to 40% of guarantee amounts. As such, a 500,000 euro guarantee will result in approximately 200,000 euros of premium income to farmers, benefiting approximately 5,000 farmer households, 25,000 family members, and sustaining approximately 12,000 hectares of certified organic land.

Challenges and Opportunities

The activities of the Triodos Sustainable Trade Fund, as with any trade finance investment strategy, are exposed to multiple risks. Triodos analyzes the risk associated with production, non-delivery, debtor, trade dispute and defaulting buyer, to name a few, in constructing their loan portfolio.

The guarantors are exposed to this risk, inherent in farming in developing countries, through TSTF as an intermediary. In the event of a natural disaster or a poor crop yield, exports to merchants will be reduced, and in turn their payments to TSTF will be reduced, and the losses charged pro rata to guarantors. Although this risk is uncorrelated with other market-related risks to which guarantors will be normally exposed, this "export risk" can be significant. Triodos has successfully mitigated these challenges due to their extensive experience and successful track record in the areas of microfinance and trade finance, as demonstrated by their management of Hivos-Triodos Fund, Triodos Doen Foundation and the Triodos Fair Share Fund. Over the past five years, according to Triodos, only two losses have been reported, amounting to less than 1% of the average amount of loans disbursed.

Guarantees with Triodos Sustainable Trade Fund represent exposure to an illiquid cash allocation. All deposits are euro-denominated, which offers an element of foreign exchange risk and/or exposure for non-EU investors. Although the investment does pay a fair cash return, it does not offer an appropriate risk-adjusted rate of return for *traditional* investors, as guarantors are not compensated beyond the interest rate on their deposit for the risks inherent in the fund. In addition, the return received in any given year is subject to any deductions from offset loans or operating losses generated by Triodos Sustainable Trade Fund.

Conclusion

For the impact investor seeking to maximize the social and environmental benefits of supporting trade finance for fair trade certified and organic goods, the Triodos Sustainable Trade Fund offers a compelling investment opportunity. Additionally, US foundations may consider qualifying, if appropriate, an allocation to the fund as a Program-Related Investment due to the fund's impact first focus.

The information presented herein has been prepared for informational purposes only and is not an offer to buy or sell, or a solicitation of an offer to buy or sell, any security or fund interest. The offering circular of each security or the respective fund's confidential offering memorandum contains important information concerning risks and other material aspects of the investment and must be read carefully before a decision to invest is made.

Although the information presented herein has been obtained from and is based upon sources we believe to be reliable, no representation or warranty, express or implied, is made as to the accuracy or completeness of that information. No assurance can be given that the investment objectives described herein will be achieved.

Background Brief

Dial 1298 for Ambulance (Dial 1298) provides a private, reliable, round-the-clock emergency ambulance response for residents in select cities within India. It utilizes a tiered pricing, cross-subsidy model to ensure access for all regardless of ability to pay. Based on the success of its Mumbai initiative, Dial 1298's principals have begun rolling out service to the top 10 cities with populations over one million within India.

Vision and Mission

Dial 1298's vision is "to assist saving human lives by becoming the leading network of life support ambulances in India." Dial 1298's mission is threefold: provide the best quality life support ambulance service as fast as possible to the patient; meet the emergency medical service needs by providing an easy to remember phone number; and provide self-employment for those with a passion to save lives.

Problem and/or Need

In India, there are more than 37 cities with one million plus population and 35 of these cities have no organized emergency medical services (EMS). Seventy-two percent of these city dwellers are estimated to have the capacity to pay for emergency medical services if available. Based on research conducted by Dial 1298, Mumbai has approximately 60,000 emergency cases per month (2,000 cases per day), 10% of which are served by ambulances. In addition, around 16,000 planned medical transfers occur on a daily basis, of which only 5% are through ambulance services. Of this potential market, Dial 1298 receives on average 50 calls a day. Other ambulance service providers in Mumbai include Nulife, Life Jet, and Ambucare. The remaining (almost 90%) of ambulance services are provided by single ambulance owners, hospitals, NGOs and government agencies.

Mumbai, location of Dial 1298's first rollout, is a city of 16 million people, yet it historically lacked any reliable ambulance or emergency medical response service. Private cars, autorickshaws, taxis or van "ambulances" with no medical equipment or trained technicians were typically used to take patients to a hospital. Without the benefit of medical personnel, these ambulances often end up functioning only as hearses. The poor suffer disproportionately from the lack of these services because they face greater transportation challenges and are less able to pay. Prior to Dial 1298, the concept of single number calling for an ambulance service was nonexistent. Also, the response time for other services was typically very high; these services were not professionally managed; and there were no communication links between the ambulances and the hospitals.

Historically and constitutionally, the provision of public health care is the state governments' responsibility. However, EMS is excluded from both the preventive care and hospital care divisions within the health care system and is grouped under Disaster Management (Department of Revenue). Thus, EMS is currently not a priority service for the government. Additionally, ambulance service is not currently covered under health insurance plans.

Business Model

Dial 1298 for Ambulance proposes to address the need of emergency medical services in the top 10 cities in India by building a fleet of ambulances managed by a 24/7 call center that will respond faster to emergency calls, cost less than the competition and provide a cleaner, better equipped and better managed service. Dial 1298 offers two types of ambulances: Basic Life Support and Advanced Life Support. All ambulances are completely equipped (suction machine, resuscitation kit, oxygen and an inventory of emergency medicine). The Advanced Life Support ambulances also offer defibrillator, ECG, cardiac monitor and portable ventilator. All ambulances are crewed with a paramedic, driver and a helper trained by programs certified by the American Heart Association and New York Presbyterian Hospital.

Tiered Pricing Cross-Subsidy Model

Dial 1298's business model is based on tiered pricing with cross-subsidies. Some customers pay less than the marginal cost of producing these goods or services, while other customers pay higher than the marginal cost.[11] A portion of the revenues generated from selling goods or services to customers able to pay the full price are used to subsidize those unable to cover any or part of the full cost of service. Dial 1298 employs a sliding price scale: wealthier customers, selecting the more expensive hospitals, pay the full rate for an ambulance ride, while the poor receive a deep discount — up to 50% off — or free service.

Dial 1298's business model targets a ratio of paid to free ambulance trips of 80 to 20. There are two classes of free transport: the transfer of road traffic accident victims to the nearest hospital and the transfer of mass casualty victims (terrorist acts, train accidents, etc.). Currently, although 20% is the upper ceiling of free or subsidized services in their business model, these types of calls equate to approximately 15% of all trips.

Growth Plans

Based on the successful rollout in Mumbai, Dial 1298 plans to scale across India by first establishing a presence in Kerala. Individuals and corporations have begun to donate ambulances to Dial 1298 as they see that this is a truly efficient and accountable way of providing life-saving emergency services to the poor. Dial 1298's model has the potential to be replicated not only in other Indian cities, but also around the world.

Dial 1298 is now being asked to bid on and is winning government contracts, something that did not exist when the firm was founded three years ago. These contracts add a new revenue stream to Dial 1298 over and above the user fee and donations from corporate sponsors for the purchase of ambulances.

Growth drivers relevant to the success of the Dial 1298 model include: increasing consumer awareness resulting in a need for a wide range of high quality emergency medical care; growth of communication technology and infrastructure; and entry of private health insurance companies to change the face of healthcare service.

Revenue drivers include: trips per day per ambulance; price charged per trip; and proportion of emergency services to basic services.

Cost Drivers include: fuel, which constitutes more than 9% of revenues; depreciation, which forms a significant part of overall costs and is presently at about 60% of total revenues (however depreciation cost will reduce to 11% of total revenues by 2011–12 as most of the capital expenses will be fully amortized); and payroll — ambulance-related salaries will account for about 21% of total revenues by 2011–12 (currently about 28%).

Financial Returns

Revenues were $1.98 million in 2008 and are expected to reach $3.3 million in 2009 and $ 3.8 million in 2010.[12] The financing dynamics for Dial 1298 involves purchasing the ambulances through the use of $1.5 million in equity obtained in 2007 from Acumen Fund, a non-profit global venture fund and one of their key investors. Acumen Fund has a significant, minority equity position in Ziqitza Health Care Limited, parent company of Dial 1298. Dial 1298 is working on a second round of funding. Acumen Fund will invest additional funds to maintain its holdings. New investors are expected to hold a minority interest and Dial 1298's founders are expected to hold less than 50% of the company.

Social Returns

While the service may need subsidies or budgetary support in rural areas, Dial 1298 appears to be fully capable of addressing the emergency medical services market needs in urban India, especially in the top 20 cities in India. As 20% of the services of Dial 1298 are estimated to be offered free of cost or at subsidized rates, this investment provides an opportunity to extend quality healthcare to a significant portion of the urban poor in India (estimated to be 5.2 to 8.7 million people in Mumbai alone). The rollout of a high-quality, affordable life-saving ambulance network in Mumbai should create a great deal of value for consumers in terms of providing adequate health care in a timely, sustainable and cost-efficient manner.

Challenges and Opportunities

Maintaining the projected customer mix will be a challenge. Dial 1298 is vulnerable if there is a precipitous drop in the percentage of fully-paid services, but the use of paid sponsors can potentially reduce this impact of a drop in paying customers. Raising capital to expand its operations may be a challenge if Dial 1298 seeks to raise capital from sources that view the lost revenues associated with the tiered pricing cross-subsidy model as reducing the prospective profitability of the company. Another possible challenge is competition that might target the higher-income portion of Dial 1298's customer base.

A major challenge ahead is education of the customer base. Even with efficient systems in place, Dial 1298 needs to educate people of all income levels about their services and the advantages of using an ambulance. The company is developing marketing campaigns to raise awareness about the importance of calling an ambulance in an emergency and effecting behavioral changes in the populace (e.g., "Save a life! Make way for an ambulance!"). Making Dial 1298's telephone number easier to recall during emergencies is also a high priority.

Finally, there are myriad marketing challenges stemming from the tiered pricing cross-subsidy model, such as selling the same level of service to different customer segments at different prices. Normally, an organization confronted with these challenges would identify different marketing campaigns for these different customer groups. However, this is difficult for an early-stage company with sparse resources.

Conclusion

Dial 1298 has successfully implemented its tiered pricing, cross-subsidy business model. It has mitigated a number of the risks and challenges delineated above through its successful efforts to receive donated capital for ambulance acquisition, and through winning government contracts. At this writing, Dial 1298 is expanding its services to other Indian urban cities.

Behavioral Finance Reflections

As previously discussed, the behavioral approach emphasizes investors' reliance on heuristics, or rules of thumb, because they do not act in a fully rational manner. Some key issues impact investors should consider when researching an impact investment include: understanding their own heuristics; being able to separate their own bias from the facts as presented; and being able to gauge if the facts as presented are fully transparent.

In the case of Triodos and Dial 1298, two investors seeing the same set of facts might come to two different conclusions. One investor might see the impact metrics as representing the best possible case, while a second investor might feel the metrics are depicting only an average scenario. What one investor may see as an opportunity in an emerging market, another may see as too high a risk to warrant an investment.

Is there a market failure stemming from representativeness bias in the Triodos and Dial 1298 business models? One could make the case that representativeness bias explains the existence of both market opportunities. This bias could also stem from excessive reliance on stereotyping, for instance, leading to a general belief that poor people are unwilling or unable to repay debt or cover ambulance fees.

11 See the University of Michigan's case study on Subsidies in Base-of-the-Pyramid Ventures, which includes a section on Dial 1298 for Ambulance: http://www.globalens.com/casedetail.aspx?cid=1428767

12 Dollar figures based on an exchange rate of 48 INR to 1 USD.

Chapter 8:

Evaluating Impact

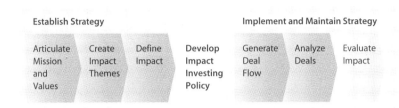

Establish Strategy

Articulate Mission and Values	Create Impact Themes	Define Impact	Develop Impact Investing Policy

Implement and Maintain Strategy

Generate Deal Flow	Analyze Deals	Evaluate Impact

Defining and Measuring Impact

As an impact investor, you are seeking the best opportunities for achieving impact within specific impact themes. With this goal in mind, how can you capture the impact of your investments and use this knowledge to drive your future strategy and investment decisions? Impact investors who are philanthropists will understand the challenges of measuring the impact of their grantmaking and recognize that similar challenges will exist with measuring the social and/or environmental benefits of impact investing.

To better understand how your impact investments are creating social and/or environmental impact, it is essential to be very clear about measurement. A key notion is to differentiate outputs from outcomes. Outputs are results you can measure or assess directly. For example, outputs for a homeownership program would include the number of housing units built or renovated. Outcomes are the ultimate changes that we are trying to make in the world. For the home-ownership program, an outcome might be increased wealth and quality of life for low-income earners. It can sometimes be difficult to evaluate whether an outcome has been achieved. Nevertheless, an organization should define its desired outcomes and work to determine how the measurable outputs correlate to those outcomes. Impact is the next link in the chain. Impact is that portion of the total outcome occurring as a result of the activity, above and beyond a predicted outcome. The following Impact Value Chain was developed as part of the Rockefeller Foundation's Double Bottom Line Project:[13]

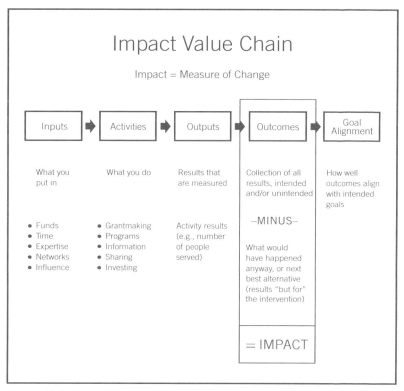

Source: Clark, Catherine, William Rosenzweig, David Long, and Sara Olsen, Double Bottom Line Project Report: Assessing Social Impact in Double Bottom Line Ventures, *the Rockefeller Foundation, 2004.*

At present, most impact investors focus on the first order derivative output of their work. This not only makes the task of measurement and reporting more feasible, it also preempts speculative and contentious debate on real causes and

Chapter 8: Evaluating Impact

effects. While impact should be measurable based on clear outcome metrics and comparable across social enterprises, we should be aware of the challenges of aggregating outputs across impact themes and overemphasizing impact themes which generate easily quantifiable outputs compared to more qualitative themes.[14] Impact investors seek to create impact assessment systems relevant to their missions while also trying to create reporting that can be compared to other investors' performance. On the financial side, setting clear benchmarks for each asset class is standard practice. Establishing the appropriate benchmarks on the impact side is not yet standardized.

Core Beliefs for Impact Assessment

Given the complexity of impact assessment, it is useful to approach this with some core beliefs. The following was developed as part of a recent McKinsey & Co Discussion Paper.[15] It focuses on foundations, but the principles apply to other impact investors as well:

- Hear the constituent voice;
- Exercise rigor within reason;
- Assess not for assessment's sake;
- Design assessment and strategy together;
- Don't let assessment sit on a shelf;
- Collaborate, don't dictate;
- Build off and build up;
- Borrow, don't reinvent; and
- Foster learning culture.

RSF Social Finance approaches the question of social impact through a holistic framework derived from the Balanced Scorecard methodology. This approach provides a roadmap for

Beartooth Capital

Beartooth Capital is a private real estate fund investing in the ranch land market to generate strong financial returns through the restoration and protection of ecologically important land. The fund focuses its work on ranch properties in the western US, working in partnership with conservation organizations and others to acquire ranches and create value through habitat restoration, land protection and ecologically appropriate, limited development. Threatened ranchland is typically protected through conservation, but conservation groups have limited resources and cannot access the capital markets. Beartooth Capital utilizes private capital to protect ecologically important ranchland, furthering the efforts of the conservation movement.

Beartooth regularly communicates investment performance and metrics related to its sustainability thesis to its investors. In their 2008 investor report, they state that they have returned approximately 27% of the capital called from investors to date, while selling less than 7% of the land the fund acquired AND:

• Followed through on their stated mission of making investments to generate competitive risk-adjusted returns for investors while achieving real conservation results;
• Protected more than 9,250 acres of the ~15,000 acres acquired to date through conservation easements or sale to conservation partners; and
• Replanted and restored more than 40 miles of creek and river by planting thousands of willows, cottonwoods and river birch and rehabilitating thousands of acres of upland habitat through rest, managed grazing and reseeding.

Source: Beartooth Capital

instilling explicit, values-based strategies and evaluation at every layer of the organization, from day-to-day business execution to client relationships to its contributions to the overall field of social finance. In terms of measuring the social impact of its lending and investment programs, RSF uses a combination of quantitative and qualitative factors with a focus on the outputs of investments such as the number of affordable housing units financed, low-income mortgages made and environmental projects initiated.

To assist prospective investors, The Calvert Foundation has created a Social Return on Investment (SROI) Calculator Tool which is available on its website. The tool allows investors to better understand potential social return on investment based on data Calvert Foundation has collected from numerous organizations in the field. For each sector, Calvert Foundation converts a potential impact investment amount into the corresponding housing units created or improved, microenterprises created, jobs created or small businesses created. The statistics are calculated based on Calvert Foundation's activities in the previous year.

Calvert Foundation also tells investors to keep the following in mind when using the tool: "Most importantly, certain program orientations, regional/country differences and other factors make it difficult to compare results of SROI calculations from group to group, region to region or social impact sector to social impact sector. It's a classic apples to oranges situation in many cases. We must keep in mind that the relative cost of creating a living wage job in San Francisco is very different from the cost of creating one in Bolivia. Likewise, if programs in one area spend a lot of resources on counseling because it is deemed necessary for the success of clients, and another region does not find it as necessary for this provision of

One Family's Approach to Microfinance and Impact

The Opus Foundation is a family foundation whose mission is to enable people to better sustain themselves, their families and communities through education and employment. The family became interested in microfinance when they made a grant to the International Rescue Committee to foster self-help and enterprise among refugees. The recipient NGO continued to send grant reports after the first year, since it had been able to recycle the original funding through the repayment it received from refugee microcredit borrowers. Intrigued by the possibility of making loans rather than grants, Opus approached the Calvert Foundation and invested in a Community Investment Note directed to international microfinance institutions in countries of interest to them as well as community development organizations where the family had businesses. When the family was considering how to leverage the foundation's philanthropic activities through impact investing, it discovered its values were clearly in alignment with those of the Calvert Foundation:

- Mutuality: Investing relationship creates mutual respect;
- Enterprise: Harnesses power of enterprise;
- Accountability: Values measurable outcomes;
- Self-reliance: 'Beneficiaries' transform their own lives;
- Self-respect: Process fosters self-confidence and dignity;
- Sustainable: Capital is returned and recycled.

Through the Community Investment Note, Opus received impact reports based on data from the microfinance institutions. Opus has also directly commissioned evaluations and developed relevant social indicators to assess the impact of their portfolio of microfinance debt and equity investments. When Opus wanted to expand their support of microfinance to include equity investments in start-up MFIs, Calvert Foundation was able to share its due diligence analysis thereby mitigating the risk of this investment. The family has since co-invested in Jamaica with several local businesses and other double bottom line investors in the start-up of a now successful microfinance institution.

social service, it can present problems in comparing social returns based on the capital amount required to produce those returns. The basic version of this tool calculates among bundles of community development organizations working in sectors or regions, so as not to lend itself to comparing one group to another."

Creating Structural Change for Measuring Impact

New systems and metrics are important for investors evaluating social and/or environmental investment options and tracking the financial and non-financial returns. The absence of standards has implications across the investment cycle:

- Potential investees (e.g., small business owners in emerging markets, clean energy companies, microfinance institutions and larger companies seeking deliberate positive social or environmental impact) do not have a clear, consistent, broadly acknowledged way to measure and communicate social impact and associated returns to potential investors;
- Intermediaries who make and facilitate new investments (e.g., social investment funds, private equity, foundations) face challenges in screening potential investees to maximize social impact of invested capital and measuring the social and environmental impact and performance at the portfolio level — requiring significant efforts to research and communicate non-financial performance; and
- Investors (e.g., foundations, private investors, institutional investors, et al) have little data with which to assess and compare performance of various funds and investees; apples to apples comparison of financial and non-financial performance lacks the standardization, transparency and rigor available for more traditional investment measures.

There are a number of initiatives under way to address the infrastructural gaps for impact assessment. In this regard, the Impact Reporting and Investment Standards (IRIS) initiative of the Global Impact Investing Network seeks to move toward standardizing the measurement and reporting of social and/or environmental impact investment. Developed by a group of leading impact investors (with support from Deloitte and Touche, PriceWaterhouseCoopers, Google.org and B Lab) and piloted with investment funds and companies around the world, the IRIS standards seek to establish uniform definitions of terms for social impact reporting (just as the GAAP standards do for financial reporting) and to equip fund managers and direct investees to adopt these standards. IRIS will also aggregate social performance data and release benchmarking reports that enable impact investors to compare investments against their peers — a capacity that proved central in the growth of mainstream venture capital and private equity.

The field of impact measurement remains very much in flux with much innovation and a lack of industry-wide standards. However, impact investors are currently deploying meaningful approaches. We anticipate that impact evaluation will continue to be an area of rapid consolidation and progress.

---

13 For additional research on impact measurement, please see the *San Francisco Federal Reserve Community Investment Review*, Summer 2009 (http://www.frbsf.org/publications/community/review/vol5_issue2/index.html).

14 See Kramer, Mark and Sarah Cooch, *Investing for Impact*, FSG Social Impact, Boston, 2006 for an analysis of impact measurement — particularly the integration of qualtitative measurements.

15 "McKinsey's Approach to Learning for Social Impact," McKinsey & Co., Discussion Paper, Draft June 2009.

Conclusion:

Coming Full Circle Using the Impact Investing Cycle

Establish Strategy				Implement and Maintain Strategy		
Articulate Mission and Values	Create Impact Themes	Define Impact	**Develop Impact Investing Policy**	Generate Deal Flow	Analyze Deals	Evaluate Impact

We hope our monograph has inspired you to move beyond the Tyranny of OR and apply the Genius of AND. Impact investing has emerged as a viable and growing discipline — across asset classes and impact themes. All types of capital can and must play a central role in moving impact investing forward. Many high net-worth individuals and foundations are putting their investment dollars where their values are with great results. However, at the end of the day, a significant share of institutional capital must move in this direction to enable this nascent movement to become mainstream. But it is not just about capital. If impact investing is to truly have an impact, it should be about systemic change, new ways of deploying capital, and capacity building of the players on both sides of the equation. What responsibility do impact investors have in solving this problem?

Rigor Matters

Impact investing is not charity. It requires and demands every bit of the same disciplined approach currently being applied to traditional investing if it is to succeed. Adding social and/or environmental criteria to existing rigorous investment evaluations may actually improve the quality and output of investments. Investors no longer need to assume that a discount be taken on their returns in order to align their investments with their impact objectives. Aligning investments with impact AND utilizing a disciplined approach is achievable.

Investment Management Best Practice

Impact investing can be done within the established parameters of investment management best practice. Impact focused financial advisors, intermediaries, investor networks and collaboratives are emerging in greater numbers. In light of the market turmoil of 2008, investments with a double or triple bottom line may be the antidote to growing mistrust in the market place and perhaps part of a new 'best practice' paradigm. While the impact investment market remains fragmented, we expect the market to grow dramatically as large asset managers enter the impact investing space.

These managers will be driven not only by clients who are increasingly demanding social and/or environmental metrics as part of their investment strategies, but also by their own values and the realization that impact investing makes good investment sense.

Impact Investment Opportunities Abound

Investment-grade impact investments are experiencing rapid growth. Global intermediaries are playing a key role in building demand for capital. These same organizations, with the help of information technology, are helping to create more fluid and transparent markets.

Approaches Are Diverse

Impact investments are bringing creative, diverse opportunities to the market. They are tapping into new markets with innovative goods and services, leveraging both social and investment capital, and providing a double or even triple bottom line return. As demonstrated by our case studies and investment profiles, impact investors continue to define their impact themes across a wide range of issue areas and theories of change without clear standardization. While this diversity can slow the development of standardized products, it provides the opportunity for impact investors to approach problem solving from a number of directions.

Money Isn't Everything

Supply and demand for capital ideally need to grow in tandem. Investors can and should play an important role in assisting the mentoring, incubation and acceleration of impact investment opportunities. Without a 'shoulder to shoulder' approach, we risk either a market where the product outpaces the investment

capital or capital is competing for product. And without open
channels between all interested parties, we risk missing
important innovation that could help move impact investing
from the sidelines into the mainstream investment market.

Understand Inefficient Markets and Use Impact Investing to Address Market Failures

Impact investing benefits greatly from consideration of
behavioral finance — not only in the assessment of investment
opportunities but also in its evolution. Awareness of behavioral
finance augments our understanding of inefficient markets,
providing a subjective lens through which we can further
evaluate a typically analytic process. Historically, impact
investing has suffered from overconfidence on the part of the
impact investing community, but also lack of confidence from
the traditional investment community. Finding an appropriate
middle ground will help move this field forward. Representative
bias is difficult to tease out, but doing so can help the
investment professionals provide more objective analysis.
Acknowledging that perceptions of trust, honesty and morality
are significant factors influencing our investment decision-
making will go a long way to co-create and sustain this brave
new world.

Take Action

And this brave new world is imperfect at best. Impact investors acknowledge this, but aren't reticent to continue experimenting, measuring and investing. And with good reason. Impact investing, for all its challenges, may ultimately prove to be the most prudent form of investing.

Appendix 1:

Impact Investment Profile Summary

The following is a list of impact investments profiles available at www.rockpa.org/impactinvesting, which were prepared in conjunction with this monograph. They are meant to serve as an illustrative example of impact investments available in the market place today and by no means represent a comprehensive list of the industry. Furthermore, additional profiles will be added online as they are completed. Please visit the site periodically for updated information.

Access Capital
Acumen Capital Markets
American River Ventures Fund II
Ariya Capital
C Change Transformative Energy and Materials Fund
China Energy Efficiency Fund
Climate Change Property Fund
Community Capital Management
Contact Fund
DWM Microfinance Fund I
E+Co People Planet Note
EcoEnterprises Fund II
EKO — Green Carbon Vehicle
Essex Investments GEOS Fund
GreenSpace Developments
Greenwood Global Tree Farm Fund
Healthpoint Services Global
Highwater Global Fund
I3 Fund
IGNIA Fund
IMPAX Environmental Markets
Innosight Ventures Fund
Living Cities Catalyst Fund

Living Forest Communities
Los Angeles Community Investment Initiative
Lyme Forest Fund III
Minlam Microfinance Africa Fund
NCB Capital Impact
Neuberger Berman Socially Responsive Equity
Pico Bonito
Planet Habitat
Rose Smart Growth Investment Fund
Root Capital
Self-Help Federal Credit Union
ShoreBank Capacity Plus Loan Program
Social Stock Exchange
Southern Bancorp
Summit Water Equity Fund
SAM Sustainable Water Strategy
USRG Power and Biofuels Fund III
Verama Agroforestry Project
WaterCredit Initiative
XPV Water Growth Equity Fund
Zouk Cleantech Europe II

See important disclaimer information on inside back cover.

Appendix 2:
Selected Bibliography

For our comprehensive bibliography please visit
www.rockpa.org/impactinvesting

Anderson, Miranda and David Gardiner, *Managing the Risks and Opportunities of Climate Change: a Practical Toolkit for Corporate Leaders*, Boston, MA CERES, 2006.

Akerlof, George A. and Robert J. Shiller, *Animal Spirits: How Human Psychology Drives the Economy, and Why It Matters for Global Capitalism*, Princeton: Princeton University Press, 2009.

Bayon, Ricardo, Amanda Hawn, and Katherine Hamilton, *Voluntary Carbon Markets: An International Business Guide to What They Are and How They Work*, 2nd ed., London: Earthscan, 2009.

Belsky, Gary and Thomas Gilovich, *Why Smart People Make Big Money Mistakes And How To Correct Them: Lessons From The New Science Of Behavioral Economics*, New York: Simon & Schuster, 1999.

Bernholz, Lucy and Lisa Richter, *Equity Advancing Equity: How Community Philanthropy Can Build Racial and Social Equity through Mission Investing*, Blueprint Research & Design and GPS Capital Partners LLC, September 2009.

Bishop, Matthew and Michael Green, *Philanthrocapitalism: How the Rich Can Save the World*, Bloomsbury Press, 2008.

Bolton, Margaret, *Foundations and Social Investment: Making Money Work Harder*, London: Esmée Fairbairn Foundation, October 2005.

Bugg-Levine, Antony, "Impact Investing Bold Models to Drive Development at Scale," *Beyond Profit*, Intellecap, May/June, pg 17-21, 2009.

Carlson, Neil, *Assessing and Managing PRI Risk: Nothing Ventured, Nothing Gained*, New York: GrantCraft Guides, 2008.

Cooch, Sarah, Mark Kramer, Fi Cheng, Adeeb Mahmud, Ben Marx, and Matthew Rehrig, *Compounding Impact: Mission Investing by US Foundations*, Boston, MA: FSG Social Impact Advisors, 2007.

Deringer, Freshfields Bruckhaus, *Legal Framework for the Integration of Environmental, Social and Governance Issues into Institutional Investment*, UNEP Financial Initiative, 2005.

Dietel, William M., *Mission Stewardship: Aligning Programs, Investments, and Administration to Achieve Impact*, New York: The F.B. Heron Foundation, 2007.

Elkington, John, and Pamela Hartigan, *The Power of Unreasonable People: How Social Entrepreneurs Create Markets That Change the World*, New York: Harvard Business School, 2008.

Emerson, Jed and Joshua Spitzer, *Blended Value Investing: Capital Opportunities for Social and Environmental Impact*, World Economic Forum, 2006.

Emerson, Jed, Joshua Spitzer and Jacob Harold, *Blended Value Investing: Innovations in Real Estate*, Oxford: Skoll Centre for Social Entrepreneurship, 2007.

Godeke, Steven, and Doug Bauer, *Philanthropy's New Passing Gear: Mission-Related Investing — A Policy and Implementation Guide for Foundation Trustees*, Rockefeller Philanthropy Advisors, 2008.

Hammond, Allen L., William J. Kramer, Robert S. Katz, Julia T. Tran, and Courtland Walker, *The Next 4 Billion: Market Size and Business Strategy at the Base of the Pyramid*, New York: World Resources Institute and International Finance Corporation/World Bank Group, 2007.

Humphreys, Joshua, *The Mission in the Marketplace: How Responsible Investing Can Strengthen the Fiduciary Oversight of Foundation Endowments and Enhance Philanthropic Missions*, Washington, DC: Social Investment Forum Foundation, 2007.

Hawken, Paul, Amory Lovins, and Hunter L Lovins, *Natural Capitalism: Creating the Next Industrial Revolution*, New York: Back Bay Book, 2000.

Kiernan, Matthew J., *Investing in a Sustainable World: Why GREEN Is the New Color of Money on Wall Street*, New York: AMACOM / American Management Association, 2009.

Krosinsky, Cary (editor) and Nick Robbins (editor), *Sustainable Investing: The Art of Long Term Performance*, Earthscan Ltd., 2008.

LaVoie, Valerie and David Wood, *Handbook on Climate-Related Investing Across Asset Classes*, Institute for Responsible Investment at the Boston College Center for Corporate Citizenship, 2009.

Passoff, Michael, *Proxy Preview 2009: Helping Foundations Align Mission and Investment*, As You Sow, San Francisco, 2009.

Segerfeldt, Fredrik, *Water for Sale, How Business and the Markets Can Resolve the World's Water Crisis*, Washington, DC, The Cato Institute, 2005.

Shefrin, Hersh, *A Behavioral Approach to Asset Pricing*, Burlington: Elsevier Inc, 2005.

Shefrin, Hersh, *Beyond Greed and Fear, Understanding Behavioral Finance and the Psychology of Investing*, Oxford: Oxford University Press, 2002.

Stetson, Anne, and Mark Kramer. *Risk, Return and Social Impact: Demystifying the Law of Mission Investing by US Foundations*, FSG Social Impact Advisors, October 2008.

A Toolkit for Foundations and Individual Investors: Harnessing Your Investments to Help Solve the Climate Crisis, CERES, Investor Network on Climate Risk and Environmental Grantmakers Association, 2008.

Wood, David and Belinda Hoff, *Handbook on Responsible Investment Across Asset Classes*, The Institute of Responsible Investing at the Boston College Center for Corporate Citizenship, 2007.

Yunus, Muhammad, *Creating a World Without Poverty — Social Business and the Future of Capitalism*, New York: PublicAffairs, 2008.

About the Authors

STEVEN GODEKE
Principal, Godeke Consulting

Steven Godeke is an independent investment advisor who works with foundations, corporations and non-profit organizations to integrate their financial and philanthropic goals. Steven advises his clients on the creation and execution of impact investment strategies across asset classes and program areas. His services include due diligence, structuring and negotiation of impact investments and portfolio performance measurement. Steven is co-author of *Philanthropy's New Passing Gear: Mission-Related Investing — A Policy and Implementation Guide for Foundation Trustees*, published in 2008 by Rockefeller Philanthropy Advisors, where he is an Affiliated Consultant. Steven is an adjunct professor at New York University's Center for Global Affairs where he currently teaches a course in Microfinance and Social Entrepreneurship.

      Prior to establishing his own firm, Steven worked for twelve years in corporate and project finance with Deutsche Bank where he structured debt and equity products and advised corporate clients in the natural resources, telecommunications, media and real estate industries. Steven grew up on a family farm in Southern Indiana and attended Purdue University where he received a B.S. in Management and a B.A. in German. He studied as a Fulbright Scholar at the University of Cologne and earned an M.P.A. from Harvard University.

RAUL POMARES
Managing Director, Springcreek Advisors, LLC

Raúl Pomares is a Managing Director of Springcreek Advisors, where he serves as the principal investment advisor to select family offices, foundations and endowments. Prior to joining Springcreek, Raúl served as a Portfolio Manager with Guggenheim Investment Advisors, where he developed integrated multi-manager portfolios for institutional and high net worth clients. In particular, Raúl applied his expertise across a broad range of impact investment themes to create an integrated manager research and portfolio construction methodology for investors. Before joining Guggenheim Partners in 2006, Raúl co-founded a boutique wealth management firm where he directed client services. He has also served as an investment advisor, international private banker and consultant on behalf of global financial institutions and private investors.

Raúl is an internationally recognized speaker and contributor to numerous publications on innovative investment solutions for return-oriented investors seeking measurable impact. He serves as Mentor – Capital Markets, for "The Global Social Benefit Incubator (GSBI™), the signature program of Santa Clara University's Center for Science, Technology and Society. Raúl received his degree in international business management from the University of San Francisco.

ALBERT V. BRUNO
William T. Cleary Professor, Leavey School of Business, Santa Clara University

Albert V. Bruno is the William T. Cleary Professor at the Leavey School of Business at Santa Clara University, where he has held a variety of administrative positions as well as founding the Center for Innovation & Entrepreneurship, and co-founding the Global Social Benefit Incubator. Professor Bruno, who earned a Ph.D. at the Krannert School at Purdue University, has taught at Harvard University as a visiting research scholar, Sup de co, Rouen, France, and at the Naval Postgraduate School. In 1982, Professor Bruno was one of 13 recipients in the US of the Leavey Foundation Award. In the same year, he was honored with the Glenn Klimek Professorship at Santa Clara, which he held for 16 years. His many articles, research publications and book chapters have been published in a diverse set of business journals and periodicals. His book, *The Market Value Process: Bridging Customer and Shareholder Value*, was republished in German in 1998.

PATRICK GUERRA
Founder and Principal, Lions Peak LLC
Co-Founder, Global Social Benefit Incubator, Santa Clara University

Patrick Guerra has served in senior management information technology, manufacturing, distribution, product management and business development roles with Hewlett Packard, AMD, PSB, Ariba and SpinCircuit, where he was President and CEO. Pat's experience includes early stage business formation and the rapid scaling of technology-based ventures. He has served on numerous academic and early-stage company boards of advisors. Pat has also served as the Executive Director, Center for Innovation and Entrepreneurship at Santa Clara University, where he co-founded the Global Social Benefit Incubator. Pat holds a B.Sc. in Economics and a M.B.A. in Operations Management and Information Systems from Santa Clara University, where he is an adjunct member of the faculty in Entrepreneurship.

Pat has done groundbreaking work with Ashoka, the Skoll and Rockefeller Foundations, and Acumen in support of the scaling and sustainability of Social Enterprises. Most recently, he has developed the Social Enterprise Innovation Network — a *purpose driven network* designed to enhance the absorptive capacity for capital of global social entrepreneurial ventures. He continues his commercial entrepreneurial pursuits as an investor and consultant to early stage technology companies as a member of the Band of Angels.

CHARLY KLEISSNER, PH.D.
Co-Founder, KL Felicitas Foundation

Dr. Charly Kleissner is a philanthropic entrepreneur utilizing his high technology background in his venture philanthropy. He is co-founder of the KL Felicitas Foundation and the Social-Impact initiative, helping social entrepreneurs worldwide to accelerate and increase their social impact. Dr. Kleissner serves on the Advisory Board of multiple not-for-profit companies like the Acumen Fund, Global Social Benefit Incubator and The Global Philanthropy Forum. He is also an advisor to multiple social venture capital funds, like MicroVest and Acumen Capital Market.

Dr. Kleissner earned his M.S. and Ph.D. in Computer Science from the University of Technology, Vienna and has over twenty years of experience as a senior technology executive in Silicon Valley working for Ariba Inc., NeXT Software Inc., Digital Equipment Corp. and Hewlett-Packard Company. Dr. Kleissner is now focusing on breaking down the barrier between the for-profit sector and the not-for-profit sector by creating and supporting social enterprises as hybrid business structures, insisting that both vehicles can be effective for achieving social change.

HERSH SHEFRIN

**Mario L. Belotti Professor of Finance,
Santa Clara University**

Hersh Shefrin is the Mario L. Belotti Professor of Finance at Santa Clara University. His book *Beyond Greed and Fear* provides a comprehensive approach to behavioral finance, and in 2009 was recognized by J.P. Morgan Chase as one of the top ten books published since 2000. Among Professor Shefrin's other works are *A Behavioral Approach to Asset Pricing*, *Behavioral Corporate Finance* and *Ending the Management Illusion*. According to a 2003 article that appeared in the *American Economic Review*, he is one of the top 15 economic theorists to have influenced empirical work. His work is in the all-time top ten downloads from the Social Science Research Network. He received his Ph.D. from the London School of Economics in 1974. He holds an honorary doctorate from the University of Oulu, Finland, and is an honorary guest professor at Central-South University in Changsha, China. Professor Shefrin is frequently interviewed by the media on financial matters.